Shared Reading
Reading With Children

Stanley L. Swartz, Rebecca E. Shook, & Adria F. Klein

With contributions by:

Cinda Moon, Karen Bunnell, Marie Belt, Debra Wakefield, and Charlene Huntley

 **Dominie Press, Inc.**

Acknowledgments

The authors would like to thank the many CELL and ExLL Literacy Coordinators, demonstration teachers and classroom teachers who assisted in the development of this book. As always we are enriched by the opportunity to work with this dedicated group of professional teachers. Foundation staff members Amie MacPherson, Cathleen Geraghty, and Laurie Roach provided important support for this project. A special thanks goes to Janet Maule Swartz for her critical review and editorial suggestions.

Publisher: Raymond Yuen
Editor: Bob Rowland
Designer: Natalie Chupil

Published by:

ᗡ Dominie Press, Inc.

1949 Kellogg Avenue
Carlsbad, California 92008 USA
www.dominie.com

ISBN 0-7685-0239-X
Printed in Singapore by PH Productions Pte Ltd
1 2 3 4 5 6 PH 04 03 02

Table of Contents

About the Authors

Dr. Stanley Swartz is professor of education at California State University, San Bernardino, and Director of the Foundation for California Early Literacy Learning, which sponsors the CELL, ExLL, and Second Chance professional development programs. Dr. Swartz is the author of the *Marine Life for Young Readers* series, co-author of *Building Blocks of Beginning Literacy*, and editor of the *Carousel Readers* and *Teacher's Choice* series, all published by Dominie Press.

Rebecca E. Shook is the Coordinator and CELL Trainer for the Foundation for California Early Literacy Learning and a Reading Recovery® Teacher Leader. She is a co-author of *Building Blocks of Beginning Literacy* and a contributor to the *Carousel Readers*. She has been an elementary teacher and principal and a county office consultant. She now divides her time between training activities and coaching teachers in their literacy efforts.

Dr. Adria F. Klein is professor emeritus of reading education at California State University, San Bernardino. Dr. Klein is the Coordinator and Trainer of ExLL and Second Chance for the Foundation for California Early Literacy Learning. She is published by Dominie Press and is the co-editor of the *Factivity* series, co-author of *Building Blocks of Beginning Literacy*, and a contributor to the *Carousel Readers*.

Dr. Swartz, Ms. Shook, and Dr. Klein recently wrote *Interactive Writing and Interactive Editing*, published by Dominie Press.

About the Contributing Authors

All of the contributing authors are Trainers for the Foundation for California Early Literacy Learning.

Cinda Moon has been a primary grades teacher for 18 years. She also has been a Reading Recovery® teacher and a CELL Literacy Coordinator.

Karen Bunnell holds a master's degree in education and has more than 16 years of experience in elementary classrooms. She also has worked as a mathematics consultant, mentor teacher, and staff developer.

Marie Belt is a reading intervention specialist for the Fontana, California School District. She has been a teacher in the primary grades for 17 years and a CELL Literacy Coordinator.

Debra Wakefield has taught primary grades in Crescent City, California for the past 25 years. She has been a Reading Recovery® teacher and currently is a CELL Literacy Coordinator in the Del Norte County School District.

Charlene Huntley has taught for 20 years in both special education and regular classrooms, ranging from early primary to nontraditional adult classrooms. She is a teacher and CELL/ExLL Literacy Coordinator in Sheridan, Wyoming.

Note to Teachers

Shared reading is an important part of a balanced literacy framework. Along with reading aloud to children and guided reading, shared reading is one of the teaching methods that we use to help children become independent readers. These three teaching methods employ various levels of teacher support, with reading aloud to children using the most support, shared reading using less, and guided reading using the least amount of support. All three teaching methods should be used each day.

Shared reading can be used in any classroom, regular, remedial, or special education, and with students of any age. It has been our experience that children enjoy the opportunity to read together with the teacher and benefit greatly from this sharing of text.

The book is organized into three parts. Part one gives instructions about the procedures employed in shared reading. Part two includes shared reading pieces and lesson plans for each reading. THESE SHARED READINGS ARE YOURS TO REPRODUCE AND USE IN YOUR CLASSROOM. Part three of the book includes a Literacy Skills Checklist, a planning document, and other additional resources. Among these resources is a guide to Writing Your Own Shared Reading. This guide is provided to help teachers create shared reading texts that meet their individual class needs.

We hope you use every opportunity to share your reading with your students, and we hope this book is useful in this important teaching method.

shared read•ing \shârd rēd ing\ n.

1: A teaching method in which the teacher and children read together from text that is visible to all.

2: A powerful way to support literacy learning in children.

1. About Shared Reading

Reading instruction in the classroom uses various levels of teacher support to help students become readers. When reading aloud, we are reading *to* children. In shared reading, we are reading *with* children. And of course, our end goal is reading *by* children as they become independent readers.

The technique of shared reading in the classroom replicates the experience of storybook reading, where the child sits on an adult's lap and listens or follows along as the adult reads aloud. In a classroom with a group of children, shared reading is done with a text format in which children can also see the print—using big books, stories, or poems copied onto chart paper, or text reproduced and displayed on overhead projector transparencies. The key is to have print large enough so that children can follow along.

Shared reading for beginning readers occurs when someone who is already a proficient reader (the teacher) reads with someone who is still learning to read (the student).

Shared reading for more proficient readers allows the teacher to focus on comprehension and introduce content area concepts, vocabulary, and advanced literacy skills.

The teacher's role in shared reading is to: 1) choose appropriate material, 2) point to the text while reading word-by-word for beginning readers, and line-by-line for more advanced readers, 3) read along with the children to support all levels of readers, 4) read in a fluent and expressive manner, 5) select explicit skills for direct instruction, and 6) observe the children's responses and behaviors to inform further teaching. The guiding principles for the selection of texts are that they fit the instructional purpose and that all children are able to see the print and hear the discussions.

> *Shared reading for beginning readers occurs when someone who is already a proficient reader (the teacher) reads with someone who is still learning to read (the student).*

SHARED READING IS:

Teacher and students reading together

When all students can see the text

Providing different levels of support

The teacher modeling reading behaviors

Providing opportunities for various instructional purposes

Discussing and clarifying how we understand what is read

Using shared reading allows the teacher to engage the students in the process of reading. Both demonstration and practice in the use of strategies and skills can be provided. Teaching that ranges from an understanding of phonology and word analysis to the use of comprehension strategies can be accomplished using shared reading. Children develop a sense of story and learn to predict not only the story sequence but also the use of language and the construction of text. Shared reading allows children the opportunity to behave like readers. By this we mean they observe a good reader and learn what good readers do when they read. The children watch how a book is handled. They see how the print is accessed. They hear the conversations about strategies that can be used to gain information from the text. Finally, they participate in the discussion about what message the author is trying to send.

Planning is an important part of getting the full value from a lesson using shared reading. The focus or purpose of the lesson should be clear in the teacher's mind. The shared reading is introduced, providing the necessary support based on what the teacher knows about the students. The teacher invites the students to join in and participate in the reading. The text is discussed, and the story or sequence of the story is retold. An important aspect of shared reading is in the discussions that accompany it. The teacher should also plan to reread the text several times and for a variety of teaching purposes. Shared reading allows for support from the teacher as a model and from other students in an appropriate learning experience. This shared model has also been found to provide access to language structure for English language learners and children with special needs.

Shared reading is a teaching method with a wide variety of uses for both beginning and proficient readers. Shared reading as a collaborative event supports the classroom built on the philosophy of developing a community of learners. The classroom community is one in which we share our learning and support the learning of one another. Shared reading helps us do both.

USES OF SHARED READING

Develop an understanding of phonology and word analysis

Demonstrate the process of reading

Use with individuals, small groups, or the whole class

Model comprehension strategies

VALUES OF SHARED READING

Provides the opportunity to model fluent and expressive reading

Provides students with the social support of the group

Provides appropriate learning experiences in content, concepts, and skills

Provides access to English language structure for English language learners

Supports oral language development of learners with special needs

2. Getting Started

Step 1

Identify an instructional purpose and choose a reading that supports the objective.

For example, if the lesson is working on beginning sounds, a shared reading of a poem that manipulates these sounds could be used.

Note: Shared reading can be used in almost all stages of literacy learning. Teachers who know what their students know can be more strategic in their use of shared reading.

The Literacy Skills Checklist (see Page 131) is recommended as one way to check children's skill levels.

Possible Teaching Points for Shared Reading are provided (see Page 139) to help guide the selection of instructional purpose.

Step 2

Arrange seating in such a way that each child can see the text.

Note: Young children using a big book or chart might sit on the floor in front of an easel.

Older children are often more comfortable staying in their seats and viewing the shared reading from an overhead projector.

Small group shared readings might be done at a table, using a table easel.

Step 3

The teacher introduces the shared reading. This introduction includes a conversation about the content of the story, the vocabulary, and any concepts or skills that the teacher thinks will make the shared reading more successful.

Note: Children can be expected to share their own ideas and experiences. Their participation should be encouraged without losing focus or the flow of the introduction.

Step 4

The teacher and the children read the shared reading together. With beginning readers, the teacher points to each word as it is read.

With more proficient readers, the teacher might point to each line of text as it is read.

The teacher should use a strong voice throughout the reading. Remember to act as a model and read with fluency and expression.

Note: With children who are just taking on the task of reading, the teacher may choose to read aloud the text first and ask the children to join in for the second reading. Remember, many children rely on the teacher's voice as a source of support.

Step 5

Reread the shared reading. Remind the children to read along.

Continue to point to each word or line of text. Use a pointer so that you do not obstruct the text.

In a subsequent reading, a child might be asked to act as the pointer.

Note: Children will join in at their own comfort level. Some might mumble or only be comfortable enough to watch. Participation will increase with each subsequent reading.

Step 6

Have a discussion about the text. Talk about the meaning of the text or the author's intent.

Try to relate this story to other readings or classroom activities.

Encourage the children to share personal experiences that can add to their enjoyment and aid their comprehension.

Note: Children should think of shared reading as fun.

Step 7

Make one or two teaching points. Too many teaching points will usually cause confusion.

Return to the instructional purpose of the shared reading and work with the children on the strategy or skill that was selected.

Ask the children to identify parts of the shared reading that illustrate a specific strategy or skill.

If a big book or chart paper is used, highlight the word or word parts with Wikki Stix® or highlighter tape. On the overhead projector, highlighting can be done with an overhead marker.

Note: Each shared reading has the potential for numerous teaching points. Different teaching points can be targeted in each subsequent reading. Revisiting the shared reading and the prior work done is very useful.

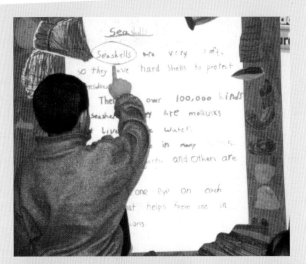

Step 8

Select shared readings from various genres.

Big books, poems, songs, chants, letters, nonfiction texts, recipes, and posters are good for shared reading, and they help children think about reading for different purposes.

Interactive writing and interactive editing tasks completed by the children are particularly useful as shared readings because of the connections that can be made to their own work.

Note: Any piece of text that everyone can see can be used as a shared reading.

Step 9

Revisit the shared readings.

Children enjoy rereading familiar material. This allows them to demonstrate proficiency and relate the prior readings to other works in progress.

Note: Reading fluently is more enjoyable than struggling with new material. Reading something with confidence is an important step in literacy learning.

Step 10

Extend the shared reading to other activities.

The children should be encouraged to read shared readings independently or in small groups.

Independent writing or interactive writing can be assigned as a follow-up to a shared reading.

More proficient readers can extend a shared reading into an interactive editing in which comprehension and the construction of new text might be emphasized.

Note: The power of shared reading is enhanced by opportunities to connect it to other elements in a balanced literacy framework. See Appendix C (Page 150) for examples of frameworks of classroom instruction for various grade levels.

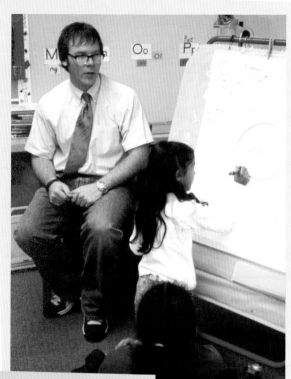

3. Shared Reading Procedures

Before the Shared Reading

Observe and Assess the Students

Instruction is most effective when teachers know what their students know. Strategic teachers are those whose teaching focuses on what they know are the needs of their students. Where are they confused? What strategies are they able to control? What are they able to do with support? What can they do independently? This information is collected through assessment and systematic observation of individual reading and learning behaviors.

Assessment of children's knowledge of phonological skills, grammar, spelling and word analysis, literary elements, and comprehension strategies should be done using a variety of assessments that are available to inform teaching. The Literacy Skills Checklist (see Page 131) is one method that can be used to track skill acquisition for each child.

Children are also observed during instruction to identify any reading confusions they might have. These observations should be systematic and recorded. The anecdotal records made on each child are cross-checked with assessment data and used to make an effective match between a child's need for support and an instructional activity.

Classroom Organization

The two major issues for organizing the classroom for shared reading are seeing and hearing. If the text is to be displayed on a chart, or if a big book will be used with a large group, students can sit on the floor close to the material. If the children are seated on the floor, make sure to allow passing room so that students can be called up for participation. An alternative might be to allow the children to bring their chairs together.

If the group is smaller, the children might sit at a table, and the text can be displayed on a table easel. When an overhead projector is being used, the students can usually stay in their seats. Grouping is an important way to engage the children in the shared reading and avoid any behavior management issues.

The materials needed for shared reading are minimal. Of primary importance is text that is either enlarged or displayed on an overhead projector. Easels, chart stands, and pocket charts are useful when using big books or printed texts. Teaching points can be highlighted using highlighter tape, Wikki Stix®, or word windows. A pointer is useful when pointing at text so that the children's view is not blocked. When using an overhead projector, a transparency marker is a good way to highlight any text that the teacher wants to give special attention.

Instructional Purpose

Shared reading is a powerful teaching method because it can be used for many teaching points. The district grade level standards should be considered as the teacher chooses the piece for shared reading. The piece should reflect the standards for language arts as well as standards for other content areas of the grade level. A shared reading is chosen for teaching points selected by the teacher (see Possible Teaching Points for Shared Reading, Page 139) as well as the teaching points that come up during the reading.

> **Materials Needed for Shared Reading**
>
> Easel, chart stand, or overhead projector
>
> Pointer
>
> Highlighter tape, Wikki Stix®, word windows, or overhead transparency marker
>
> Magna Doodle® or white board
>
> Alphabet chart
>
> Name chart
>
> Word wall

Text Selection

Text selection involves numerous considerations. In choosing material for a shared reading, consider the type of reading planned and the instructional objectives. The students may or may not have knowledge of the content. This will affect how the book is introduced. Curriculum content, language structures, vocabulary, and interest appropriate to the age of the students are important when choosing a piece for shared reading. In a read aloud, the teacher does all of the reading and can select text that has language structures that are above those of the children. In shared reading, the teacher and students share the reading of the text, so language structure and vocabulary should reflect those of the students. The majority of the vocabulary and word usage in the text should be within the children's understanding. During the reading, there is extensive discussion and

> **What Happens Before the Shared Reading**
>
> Understand students' strengths.
>
> Recognize students' interests.
>
> Know the grade level standards.
>
> Examine possible reading texts.
>
> Plan how to execute the lesson.

interaction about the text itself and the intent of the author in writing the text. During shared reading, children extend their reading skills, build their knowledge of the content area, and become more interested in realizing what they know about a subject. As they become more proficient and build new knowledge about a subject, they can use a variety of genre. Fiction, nonfiction, and poetry will encourage conversation about the subject and build the students' knowledge of the text type. Text selection should balance subject and student interest with skills that can be addressed in the text.

Introducing a New Shared Reading

Proficient readers provide themselves with their own introduction prior to reading a text. They may know the author of the text they have chosen. They may read the inside cover or the back of the book jacket to grasp a synopsis of the book. Proficient readers may read book reviews or look at the bestsellers list to choose a book. Even friends and family members may provide a sort of introduction by talking about a book they have read; a proficient reader may make a decision based on their recommendations. Some proficient readers choose a book by reading the first or last page or chapter before deciding on a text. Younger readers do not have all of these resources to help them decide on a book or to help them determine what a book is going to be about.

The teacher must determine how much of an introduction is needed for the specific group of individual children for the book to be shared. How much background knowledge do they have of the subject area? What kind of strategies do they have to determine if their attempts are accurate? Are they able to pay attention to their own reading and determine if their reading is making sense to them and sounding the way language usually sounds in books? Are they able to analyze the print to determine if the features of print, or the letters and combinations of letters, look like the words they are reading?

Shared Reading Text Selections

Big books	Charts
Excerpts from content area texts	Journal articles
	Maps
Magazine articles	Recipes
Newspapers	Math story problems
Reader's theater scripts	Cartoons
Poems	Interactive editing
Interactive writing	Tables
Graphs	Manuals
Lists	Pamphlets
Menus	Pocket charts
Outlines	Multiple copies of text
Songs	

Sample Book Introductions

This example demonstrates how introductions differ, based on the amount of support needed by a group of children.

The example uses the book *The Clock That Couldn't Tell Time*. It could be used for a unit on learning how to tell time or a science unit about the rotation of the earth around the sun.

High Support

The teacher begins by saying the title of the book and showing the children the cover of the book, which features an old grandfather clock with a big smile on his face and musical notes surrounding him. The teacher tells the students that the clock was chiming his musical sounds and it looked like he really enjoyed his job. But since the title is *The Clock That Couldn't Tell Time*, there is an opportunity for the students to predict what that title might mean. The teacher would then begin to look at and discuss with the children each picture in the book, eliciting ideas from them, based on the pictures. The teacher's job during a highly supportive introduction is to guide the discussion to information that is relevant to the story in the text. The important parts of each page are detailed here.

When I was a young boy,
we lived in a small yellow house.
It was just big enough for us
and our grandfather clock. 3

The clock stood proudly
in his own little corner
of the living room. 4

From there, he could look out
our east window.
As soon as the sun went by,
the clock began to chime. 5

Page 3: The little boy in the story is telling us that his family lived in the small yellow house that can be seen in the picture. The family had an old grandfather clock that we had seen on the cover of the book.

Pages 4-5: The clock was beside a window in the living room, where he was able to see the sun go by each day. When he saw the sun, he began to chime.

He knew it was morning.
His chime echoed
throughout the house. 6

We knew it was time
to get up. 7

Then, one day,
we were driving through the country. 8

We saw the prettiest white house
with blue shutters.
It was for sale. 9

Pages 6-7: When the family heard the clock chime echo throughout the house, they knew that it was morning and that it was time to get up.

Pages 8-9: On these pages, we can see that the family is in a car driving through the country when they see a house for sale. They thought it was the prettiest house with blue shutters.

We loved the house,
so we bought it.
Everybody and everything
moved in. 10

There was a problem.
Where were we going to put
our grandfather clock? 11

We put him in the hall,
but he seemed sad.
Our grandfather clock didn't
stand as proudly as before. 12

He missed his window.
How could he tell
what time it was? 13

Pages 10-11: The family bought the house and moved in with everything they owned, including the grandfather clock. But if you look at Dad, you can tell by the question mark and the look on his face, and by the way he is holding out his hands, that he doesn't know where to put the grandfather clock.

Pages 12-13: They put the grandfather clock in the hall, but he doesn't look very happy there, does he? He's not standing as proudly as he did before, is he? What do you think may be wrong with him? Could it be that he misses his window? Do you think he can still tell time?

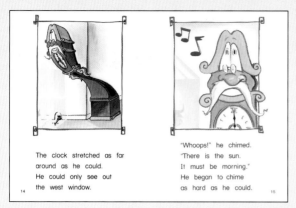

The clock stretched as far around as he could. He could only see out the west window.
14

"Whoops!" he chimed. "There is the sun. It must be morning." He began to chime as hard as he could.
15

Page 14: Look at the grandfather clock stretched around the corner toward the window. What do you think he is trying to do?

Page 15: On this page, the grandfather clock finally saw the sun, and he began to chime.

But everyone was already up. "What happened to the clock?" we cried.
16

"What did I do wrong?" wondered the clock. He felt so ashamed, he no longer chimed.
17

Pages 16-17: Everyone is looking at the grandfather clock because they were already up! They probably think something is wrong with the clock. Look at the grandfather clock. Do you think he might be ashamed because he chimed at the wrong time? Why do you think he chimed?

We decided the hall was no place for a handsome grandfather clock.
18

We moved tables, chairs, and lamps. Finally we found a perfect spot facing the east window.
19

Pages 18-19: The family decided to move everything around so that the grandfather clock could be in the perfect spot facing the east window. That way, he could see the sun come up. Look at father and mother moving all the things in the picture. What things did they have to move?

Now our grandfather clock could look out the right window.
20

When he saw the sun, he would know it was morning, because the sun comes up in the east and goes down in the west.
21

Pages 20-21: Now the grandfather clock could look out and see the sun come up in the east each morning.

The next day our clock saw the sun go by. He began to chime.
22

He chimed more proudly than ever.
23

Pages 22-23: Doesn't the grandfather clock look proud, now that he is chiming at the right time of day?

And sure enough, it was morning.
24

Page 24: Is it the right time of day? How can we be sure?

Average support

An introduction for a group of more fluent readers who collectively have many strategies in place would still try to provide the central idea of the story and encourage the children to look through the book to develop an understanding of the story prior to the shared reading. This introduction would be less supportive and include less information.

In this story, The Clock that Couldn't Tell Time, there is an old grandfather clock that chimes every morning and wakes up the family that owns him when the sun comes up. But one day the family moves to a new house, and there doesn't seem to be a good place for the grandfather clock. They put him in the hall, but he can't see the sun early in the morning, so he chimes at the wrong time of day, after everyone is already up. He is so ashamed that he stops chiming altogether! Finally, they move him close to a window that faces east where he can see the sun come up early in the morning. Once again, he begins chiming and waking everyone up. He is so proud of himself because he does the job that the family needed him to do.

The teacher may choose specific pictures for the children in the group to look at prior to the first reading.

Pages 4-5: Discuss how the grandfather clock is proudly standing in his corner, that the sun is going by the window, and that we can see that the grandfather clock is chiming.

Pages 8-9: Discuss the fact that this is the new house and what that might mean for the grandfather clock.

Pages 12-13: Discuss how sad the grandfather clock is and why he is not as proud as he used to be.

Pages 18-19: Discuss how the family is moving things around in order to find a window facing east for the grandfather clock.

Pages 22-23: Discuss how proudly the grandfather clock chimes, now that he is facing the right way and can see the sun go by each morning.

Low Support

Children who need very little support in collectively reading this level text would probably be able to be given an introduction even less supportive than the one given to the middle group.

Looking at the cover and reading the title of the book, the teacher might ask the children to make predictions based only on this little bit of information. Sometimes that is all readers have to go on before they begin reading.

Beginning of Book
In this story, The Clock that Couldn't Tell Time, there is an old grandfather clock that chimes every morning and wakes up the family that owns him when the sun comes up. But one day the family moves to a new house, and there doesn't seem to be a good place for the grandfather clock. What do you think might happen next?

As the children read the text with the teacher, they will be able to confirm or discount their predictions and then, clarifying their ideas, make further predictions.

Before pages 12 and 13
They put him in the hall, but he can't see the sun early in the morning, so he chimes at the wrong time of day, after everyone is already up. He is so ashamed that he stops chiming altogether! So, what do you think might happen now?

Again the process continues, allowing the children the opportunity to clarify their current ideas and make further predictions.

Before pages 18-19
Finally, they moved him closer to a window that faces east where he can see the sun come up early in the morning. Once again, he begins chiming and waking everyone up. He is so proud of himself because he does the job that the family needed him to do.

Ask questions to assist the children in summarizing the story.

During the Shared Reading

Teaching Points

Many teaching points can be made during a shared reading. Some of these teaching points are planned by the teacher prior to the reading. Others come up during the reading as the teacher and children discuss the text.

Alphabetic Principle

Alphabetic principle is known to be the important beginning point for emergent readers, and a concept that requires continuous reinforcement for struggling readers. Letter-name and letter-sound correspondence need special attention for work with English language learners.

Alphabetic Principle

Letter recognition

Letter formation

Letter-name correspondence

Letter-sound correspondence

Alphabetic order

Concepts About Print

Directionality

One-to-one matching

Return sweep

Spacing, indentation, paragraph form, charts, and text layout

Concept of first and last parts of words, sentences, and stories

Punctuation, reading the punctuation

Concepts About Print

Reading is a learned skill and as such needs specific support. The early support needed by children includes how we use books and how we access other sources of print. Children need direct instruction in the skills needed to handle print and understand the written page.

Phonemic Awareness and Phonics

Hearing sounds in words

Inflectional endings

Rhyming

Syllabication

Compound words

Onset and rime

Segmentation

Chunking and blending

Root words

Sounds in sequence

Analogies

High frequency words

Spelling patterns

Consonants, blends, short and long vowels, digraphs, diphthongs

Alliteration

Suffixes, prefixes, root words

Phonemic Awareness and Phonics

There is universal agreement that phonemic awareness and phonics are critical to the development of reading. Less certain is the best way to teach these concepts. Shared reading is an opportunity to make these important teaching points while reading a book. Teaching connected to immediate need is likely to be more powerful than teaching skills not connected to a reading task.

Written Language Conventions

What we find in text can be complicated. Children need the opportunity to learn about language and how it is used in writing. Shared reading provides access to text that is more difficult than text the child can read alone and gives teachers an appropriate forum for reviewing written language conventions.

Written Language Conventions

Punctuation and capitalization

Spelling and word analysis

Sentence structure

Grammar

Parts of speech

Word usage

Irregular words

Onomatopoeia

Contractions

Metaphors, similes

Idioms

Advanced Reading Skills

Beyond developing the skills of the beginning reader is the expectation that children will become more proficient and independent in their reading. The goal is a reader who can decode, read with fluency, and comprehend the text. Shared reading is a teaching method that supports the transition to independence.

Advanced Reading Skills

Fluency

Text structure

Word study

Comprehension

    Predicting

    Understanding the main idea and themes

    Summarizing

    Cause and effect

    Inferring

    Synthesizing

Procedures

Read the Text Aloud

The teacher may choose to first read the text alone while the students listen, or invite the students to join in and read along. The teacher may choose to point word-by-word, point to the beginning of each line, or point to the beginning of the text, depending on reader proficiency. The teacher's voice should be clear, strong, and constant. The children join in at varying levels. This gives them the chance to behave like readers, but with the support of the teacher and the rest of the class.

The teacher should encourage conversation throughout the initial reading. This will allow the students to use their background knowledge and make various connections.

In the initial readings and subsequent rereadings, the teacher serves as a model. The teacher can discuss a broad selection of behaviors that are used by good readers. Throughout the shared reading, the teacher should be fluent and expressive. The teacher discusses book language and how it differs from the way we speak, and models reading strategies and aids to comprehension.

> ### What to Model in Shared Reading
>
> *Fluent, expressive reading*
> *The nature of book language*
> *Reading strategies*
> > *Self-monitoring*
> > *Problem-solving*
> > *Cross-checking*
> > *Self-correcting*
> *Comprehension*
> > *Making connections within and beyond the text*

Reread the Text

Reread the piece enough times so that children become familiar with meaning, vocabulary, and the structure of language. The teacher's voice remains constant, even as the text becomes familiar to the students. The students should be encouraged to take part in conversations focusing on ideas that are different than those discussed during the first reading.

Revisit, Reread, and Reteach

This is how shared reading progresses over time. Revisit the text for a variety of teaching points and reasons throughout the year. This gives the students a chance to connect what they have learned and apply it at higher levels as they make progress and become more proficient. As with anything that is read, repeated rereading allows for different teaching points while allowing children to read with fluency. Comprehension becomes a primary focus in the revisit, reread, reteach process.

After the Shared Reading

After the shared reading, the teacher engages the children in a discussion. The teacher chooses various teaching points that should cross both content area and language arts standards. Comprehension and skills can be discussed orally, but they might be best reinforced by asking the students to highlight or point to text that illustrates the discussion point.

> ### What Happens During the Shared Reading
>
> *Read text aloud*
> *Reread text*
> *Instruct*
> *Revisit, reread, reteach*

This process can be repeated after each reading, with new teaching points building on those from prior readings and discussions.

The discussion sessions after the shared reading might focus on teaching an explicit skill or on various word attack skills. The discussion can be used to promote accurate spelling and vocabulary. The opportunities are endless, and teachers are encouraged to focus on the needs of their students.

Independent Reading

After many rereadings, most shared readings can be used for independent reading during free choice reading time. Children who needed support in early readings are now able to handle the text by themselves. These books can be kept in an independent reading area, or they might be incorporated into a literacy center.

Interactive Writing

In interactive writing, the teacher and the students negotiate the text and then share the pen to create a piece of writing. Shared reading is an opportunity to use the content or skill area from a reading and then extend the work into a writing task. A poem that is shared might be used to generate a new poem composed by the students. The interactive writing can then be used as a shared reading.

Interactive Editing

Interactive editing is a process in which the teacher and the students work together to edit text into new formats. A shared reading could be interactively edited by identifying key content words in the passage, paraphrasing the material, and then writing new and original text. The new piece could be used for a shared reading.

Independent Writing

Both interactive writing and interactive editing can be used as transition writing methods to encourage higher level independent writing. Students are encouraged to connect what they have read together in shared reading to a cooperative writing activity like interactive writing or interactive editing, and then

take this new information and learning to their own writing. As an example, in both interactive writing and interactive editing, students might be encouraged to change the writing type or genre. A story might become a poem, or a poem might become a reader's theater script.

Curricular Extensions

Shared readings with content focus are available in most curriculum areas. Teaching that carries content and helps children become more proficient readers at the same time is an efficient use of teaching time. It helps children understand reading for different purposes and the use of comprehension strategies in the content areas.

Shared Readings
You Can Use

Lesson Plans Included

Let's Learn Words

Words, words on the wall,

What's the fairest word of all?

Is it big or is it small?

Is it short or is it tall?

Can you stretch it very long?

Can you sing it like a song?

Close your eyes and turn around.

Quiet now, don't make a sound.

_____ is the work I pick.

Let's learn how to spell it, quick.

First, take a look at all the letters,

This will help to spell it better.

Can you see it in your head?

Take a picture of the word I said.

Open your eyes, now look and see,

Write it quickly, one, two, three!

Now check it out, let's all see,

Did you spell it correctly?

Shared Reading 1
Let's Learn Words

Area of Study
Language Arts

Title of Shared Reading
Let's Learn Words
By Cinda Moon and Debra Wakefield

Text Structure
Poetry

Primary Purpose
To reinforce steps in learning to spell a word
To introduce strategies for spelling
To provide practice for students to monitor known high frequency words

Lessons
First Reading Focus:
To Develop Understanding

- Prepare for this text by having several known high frequency words written on individual word cards to place in the interactive part of the text.

- Read the title of the text and invite the students to make predictions about the content.

- Reread the text several times to internalize the rhythm and become familiar with the content.

- Reread the text one line at a time and develop movements that describe the words.

Additional Readings:
To Develop Strategies and Skills

Strategies
- Ask the students if the ideas in the text will help them when they are learning to spell words. Ask them to restate the spelling strategies from the text in their own words.

- Reread the text and discuss how difficult it is to point word by word with a text that we read quickly and fluently. Tell the students how their eyes must take over the task of reading and keeping place within the lines. Demonstrate how to point to the left side of the text, read across to the right, using only the eyes, and then moving the finger down to the next line of text in order to keep place.

- Reread the selection and locate known words in the text. Reinforce how these anchor words help the eyes read across the lines of print.

Skills
- Reread the poem to reinforce the principle of onset and rime, using any of the common onsets and rimes found in the

text (*wall*, *all*, *small*, *tall*, *long*, *song*, *around*, *sound*, *pick*, *quick*, *letter*, *better*, *see*, and *three*).

- Reread the text. Look at rhyming words that sound the same but do not look the same, (*head*, *said*, and *see*, *correctly*). Discuss spelling patterns.

- Reread the text. Locate and highlight various punctuation marks. Demonstrate and model fluent reading, using punctuation.

Future Readings:
Other Possible Teaching Points
- Use the poem when learning additional high frequency words.

- Locate and highlight words that are plural.

- Highlight number words (*one two*, *three*) and discuss why words are written out rather than used as the number symbol.

Classroom Extensions
- Create a literacy center by making individual word cards, using words from the word wall. Reread the poem, using a variety of words.

- Ask the students if the style of the text reminds them of another author's style of writing. Explore texts by Dr. Suess and make comparisons.

Additional Resources
Falwell, C. *Word Wizard*. Clarion Books, 1998. ISBN 0395855802

Scarry, R. *Best Word Book Ever*. Western Publishing, 1980. ISBN 0307155102

Tobias, T. *A World of Words*. Lothrop, Lee & Shepard Books, 1998. ISBN 0688121292

Let's Listen!
Let's Read!
Let's Write!

The more we practice listening,
Our listening, our listening,
The more we practice listening,
The better we'll be.
For you listen and I listen,
And they listen and we listen.
The more we practice listening,
The better we'll be!

The more we practice reading,
Our reading, our reading,
The more we practice reading,
The better we'll be.
For you read and I read,
And they read and we read.
The more we practice reading,
The better we'll be!

The more we practice writing,
Our writing, our writing,
The more we practice writing,
The better we'll be.
For you write and I write,
And they write and we write.
The more we practice writing,
The better we'll be!

Sing to the tune of "The More We Get Together"

Grades K-1

Shared Reading 2
Let's Listen! Let's Read! Let's Write!

Areas of Study
Language Arts, Social Studies

Title of Shared Reading
Let's Listen! Let's Read! Let's Write!
By Nadine Haddock

Text Structure
Song

Primary Purpose
To excite students about listening, reading, and writing

To add music to a text in order to make the text more accessible to all students

Lessons
First Reading Focus:
To Develop Understanding
- Display the illustrated text. Before reading, ask the students to talk about what the students in the illustrations are doing. Tell them that pictures displayed in books or other kinds of text are there to help us predict and understand what the text is about.

- Read the text. Make connections to the predictions the students have made and to the new information provided by the text.

Additional Readings:
To Develop Strategies and Skills

Strategies
- Sing the song, one stanza at a time. Ask the students to think about different times during the day that they listen, read, and write. Engage them in conversation about the things they like best in school. Take pictures of students as they engage in the activities described in the text and display them with the text.

- Sing the song, and locate and highlight different high frequency words, such as *we, an, the, you,* and *our.* Discuss how these words occur often in print and that they need to be read quickly and easily, without even thinking. Add the words to the word wall and locate examples of each one throughout the text.

Skills
- Sing the text, and locate and highlight all words that have the *–ing* ending. Go back to the text and locate the root words for each one. Using a Magna Doodle®, write each root word with the *–ing* form beneath it. Demonstrate how adding *–ing* changes words into new words.

Future Readings:
Other Possible Teaching Points
- Locate a variety of words in the text. Say them and clap out the number of syllables in the words.

Classroom Extensions
- Use interactive writing to extend this song, using the same pattern.

- Create a class book that has the text of the song, along with any newly written text. Place each stanza on a different page and have the students add illustrations.

- As you teach high frequency words, ask the students to search for those words in other texts displayed in the classroom. Highlight those words.

Additional Resources
Cain, J. *The Way I Feel.* Parenting Press, Inc., 2000. ISBN 1884734715

Carlson, N. *I Like Me.* Penguin Putnam Books, 1990. ISBN 0140508198

Lansky, B. *No More Homework! No More Tests!* Simon and Schuster Trade, 1997. ISBN 0671577026

Please, Mr. Sun

Please come out here, Mr. Sun.
_____ and I
Want to have some fun.

We do not want another storm.
_____ and I
Want to be nice and warm.

Come and chase the rain away.
_____ and I
Want to go out and play.

Don't let the North Wind blow.
_____ and I
Won't know where to go.

Mr. Sun, what can we say?
_____ and I
Want a beautiful day.

Shared Reading 3
Please, Mr. Sun

Areas of Study
Language Arts, Science

Title of Shared Reading
Please, Mr. Sun
By Debra Wakefield

Text Structure
Poetry

Primary Purpose
To introduce students to monitor their reading with names as known words

To introduce students to a study of weather

Lessons
First Reading Focus:
To Develop Understanding

- Prepare the text on a chart or on sentence strips in a pocket chart. Put the students' names on individual word cards to place in blanks.

- Reread the text several times, changing the names that are displayed in the text each time.

Additional Readings:
To Develop Strategies and Skills

Strategies

- After rereading the text, ask the students to locate the names of their classmates in the poem. Discuss how names are words, and that when we read, we can look for words that we know. Reread, point to each word clearly, and pause at the names in the poem. Point out that our voices must match the text.

- After rereading the text, have the students locate other words they know. Highlight high frequency words such as *I*, *and*, *to*, *the*, and *can*. Discuss how known words help readers monitor and ensure that what has been read is correct.

Skills

- Locate the words *I* and *a* in the text. Discuss how these are the only two words in the English language that are spelled with just one letter. Reinforce the difference between a letter and a word and how we know that words have spaces that come before and after the group of letters.

- Locate all the words in the poem that are names. Discuss how names always begin with a capital letter. Reinforce the concept of first letter by highlighting the capital letter of each name.

Another way to use students' names.

Future Readings:
Other Possible Teaching Points

- Locate and chart all the words in the poem that contain the letter *a*. Sort them according to sound.

- Use magnetic letters to demonstrate the concept of onset and rime with the words *say*, *day*, *play*, and *away*. Ask the students to think of other words that can be made, using the *–ay* rime.

Classroom Extensions

- Create a literacy center, using this poem displayed in a pocket chart. Have the students manipulate and read the chart, changing the names.

- Interactively write what the students like to do on rainy days and illustrate their work for a class book.

- Graph the weather daily.

Additional Resources

Eagle, K. *It's Raining, It's Pouring*. Whispering Coyote Press, 1994. ISBN 1879085712

Rogers, P. *What's the Weather Like Today?* Scholastic, Inc., 1989. ISBN 0590450131

Bayer, J. A *My Name is Alice*. Penguin Putnam Books, 1987. ISBN 0140546685

Brandley, F. *Sunshine Makes the Seasons*. HarperCollins Children's Books, ISBN 0064450198

Saunders-Smith, G. *Sunshine*. Capstone Press, 1998. ISBN 1560657804

Slate, J. *Miss Bindergarten Gets Ready For Kindergarten*. Penguin Putnam Books, 2001. ISBN 014056273

Head, Shoulders, Knees, and Toes

Head, shoulders, knees, and toes.
Knees and toes.

Head, shoulders, knees, and toes.
Knees and toes.

And eyes, and ears, and mouth,
And nose.

Head, shoulders, knees, and toes.
Knees and toes.

Grades
K-1

Shared Reading 4
Head, Shoulders, Knees, and Toes

Area of Study
Language Arts

Title of Shared Reading
Head, Shoulders, Knees, and Toes

Text Structure
Song

Primary Purpose
To allow students to practice naming body parts

To provide the opportunity for students to match their voices to text, using a familiar song as a support

Lessons
First Reading Focus:
To Develop Understanding

- Have the students become familiar with the selection by singing the song many times without the printed copy available.

- Introduce the text by having the students locate their own body parts. Have them imitate the movements described in the text by touching their heads, shoulders, knees, and toes. Ask them to make predictions about what the text might say.

- Read the text, inviting the students to join in. Point carefully to each word while reading. The students may notice at this time that the words are familiar.

- Sing the text. On subsequent readings, speed up and read faster with each verse.

Additional Readings:
To Develop Strategies and Skills

Strategies

- Reread the text and tell the students that the text is an example of familiar words they know how to write. Talk about words, and how they are represented on a page by using letters along with spaces that delineate word boundaries. Demonstrate how each spoken word corresponds to one word on the page by pointing crisply under each word on the page as it is spoken.

- Reread the text and ask the students to find the high frequency word *and*. Highlight the word, using Wikki Stix® or highlighter tape. Talk to the students about the importance of locating words they know in text. Tell them that these words can help them know they are reading the text accurately.

Skills

- Look at the words *head*, *shoulders*, *knees*, and *toes*. Discuss that *head* refers to one body part, while the others refer to plurals. Talk about the fact that the *s* at the end of those words makes them plural. Look at *eyes*, *ears*, *mouth*, and *nose*. Decide if these are singular or plural.

- Look at the word *shoulders*. Discuss that the first sound of that word is spelled with two letters. Ask the students to orally generate a list of other words that begin with the same sound. Choose one that is a high frequency word, such as *she*, to add to the word wall and use as a reference for that sound.

Future Readings:
Other Possible Teaching Points

- Have the students locate examples of words in the text that are the same. Talk about the fact that words that are the same have the same letters, written in the same order.

- Highlight different words in the text. Find the names of students in the class that share the same initial sound.

Classroom Extensions

- Have the students illustrate themselves performing the different parts of the song. Post these illustrations alongside the text.

- Use interactive writing to label the body parts of a life-size figure of a student. Post this figure alongside the lyrics of the song.

- Use interactive writing to write an innovation of the text, using different body parts.

Additional Resources
Arnold, T. *Parts*. Penguin Putnam Books for Young Readers, 2000. ISBN 0140565337

Arnold, T. *More Parts*. Dial Books for Young Readers, 2001. ISBN 0803714173

Barnes, K. *How It Works: The Human Body*. Barnes and Noble Books, 1997. ISBN 0760704287

Eenie, Meanie, Minie, Moe

Eenie, Meanie, Minie, Moe!

There's so much for me to know.

I'm working hard from head to toe,

To think and stretch and learn and grow.

I know that when I read a book,

It's important to think, while I look.

I think about what the pictures show,

And what the author wants me to know.

I have to listen to what I say,

And ask myself if it sounds okay.

Does it sound like language I have heard,

Or do I need a different word?

I know that if I take a guess,

My reading will really be a mess.

It's the meaning that I have to catch,

But I also have to make the letters match.

Now, if I am really smart,

I will blend together every part.

There's so much more I need to know,

Than Eenie, Meanie, Minie, Moe!

Shared Reading 5
Eenie, Meanie, Minie, Moe

Area of Study
Language Arts

Title of Shared Reading
Eenie, Meanie, Minie, Moe
By Debra Wakefield

Text Structure
Poetry

Primary Purpose
To remind students of the different strategies they can use when they read

Lessons
First Reading Focus:
To Develop Understanding

- Familiarize the students with the oral traditional poem "Eenie, Meanie, Minie, Moe" as a game to choose tasks. Use it often before introducing this shared reading innovation.

- Read the title of the shared reading aloud. Ask the students to think of the game as they read the new version together. Compare and contrast the two versions. The students should be familiar with reading strategies before using this poem.

- Discuss the text and how it may help the students help themselves when reading.

Additional Readings:
To Develop Strategies and Skills

Strategies
- Reread the text and choose a word that contains a common rime, such as *make*. Demonstrate with a Magna Doodle® how knowing a part of a word may help solve other words. Write *make* and demonstrate how knowing the *–ake* part can help problem-solve words such as *snake, cake, flake*, etc. when reading.

- Find other words in the text for students to figure out by using a part they know.

- Reread the text, one stanza at a time. Ask the students to restate the main idea in their own words. Discuss how the ideas from the poem have helped them while they read.

Skills
- Reread the text and listen for words that rhyme. Highlight the words and note how rhyming words sometimes contain similar spelling patterns (*Moe/toe, know/grow*), but not always (*heard/word, know/Moe*).

- Reread the text and locate words with the *ea* spelling pattern. Discuss the differences between the sounds heard in the words *Meanie, head*, and *learn*.

Future Readings:
Other Possible Teaching Points

- Reread the text and prompt a discussion about rhyming words and where they occur in the text. Demonstrate how knowing about this type of structure helps in making predictions of words that are on the ends of each line.

- Reread the text to locate all contractions. Talk about what contractions mean and how we read them. Remind the students to "Make it match," when they read so they read *I'm* rather than *I am*.

Classroom Extensions
- Interactively write a list of strategic prompts for the students to use as a resource when problem-solving unknown words.

- Create a poetry notebook to collect individual copies for independent reading.

Additional Resources
Bunting, E. *The Wednesday Surprise*. Clarion Books, 1989. ISBN 0899197213

Bloom, B. *WOLF!* Orchard Books, 1999. ISBN 0531301559

Bradley, M. *More Than Anything Else*. Orchard Books, 1995. ISBN 0531094642

I Can Write a Letter

First, I start with the date,
So I won't send it late.

Then to bring some good cheer,
I start my letter with "Dear."

Next, I write my own note,
And my pen seems to float.

Until I get to the end,
And I sign it, "Your friend."

12-24-01

Dear Santa,

I can't wait until you get here! Don't forget to wake me when you arrive!

Your friend,

John

Shared Reading 6
I Can Write A Letter

Area of Study
Language Arts

Title of Shared Reading
I Can Write a Letter
By John Young

Text Structures
Poetry, Friendly Letter

Primary Purpose
To teach early reading behaviors and strategies
To teach students the parts of a friendly letter

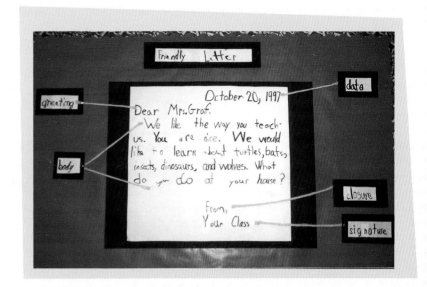

Lessons
First Reading Focus:
To Develop Understanding

- Ask the students to look at the format of the letter and make predictions about what the text may be about and the reason the text is arranged in a different way.

- Read together the letter to Santa and hold a discussion about what the author chose to write in the letter. Discuss alternative ideas that interest the students. Establish that the students will be writing their own letters, and that this text will serve as an example. Discuss how letters have specific parts that are always included.

- Read "I Can Write a Letter" together. Discuss how this will help the students write their own letters correctly.

- Reread the text several times and talk about any unfamiliar words or phrases (*cheer, pencil seems to float*).

Additional Readings:
To Develop Strategies and Skills

Strategies
- Use a pointer when rereading the text. Point carefully under each word, giving each word one crisp point. Read slowly but fluently.

- Reread the text and use a masking card to isolate words and letters, discussing the difference between the two.

- At the end of each line, ask the students where they should read next. Use a pointer to demonstrate the concept of return sweep, modeling while rereading with the students. Ask individual students to be the pointer during rereading.

Skills
- Reread the text and listen for words that rhyme. Look at the rhyming words and discuss whether they look the same.

- Demonstrate onset and rime with the words *date* and *late*. Show how these words can make other words such as *fate, mate, plate* and *skate*.

Future Readings:
Other Possible Teaching Points

- Reread the text to locate and identify commas. Highlight the commas and discuss how they help us to read fluently. Demonstrate fluent reading, teaching that a comma indicates a pause in our reading voice. Reread the text, emphasizing the pause.

- Reread and use this text as an example for organizing writing with ordering words, *first, then, next*.

Classroom Extensions
- Become pen pals with students in another class.

- Have the students independently write their own letters.

- Establish a letter-writing center.

Additional Resources
Ahlberg, J. & A. *The Jolly Pocket Postman*. Little, Brown and Co. 1995. ISBN 0-316-60202-7

Adler, B. *Children's Letters to Santa Claus*. Card Publishing Co., 1993. ISBN 1559721960

Ahlberg, A. *The Jolly Postman: Other People's Letters*. Little, Brown and Company, 1986. ISBN 0316020362

Ahlberg, A. *The Jolly Christmas Postman*. Little Brown Children's Books, 2001. ISBN 0316127159

James, S. *Dear Mr. Blueberry*. Aladdin Paperbacks, 1991. ISBN 0689505299

Prelutsky, J. *It's Christmas*. Greenwillow Books, 1981. ISBN 0688004393

What Is Good for Me?

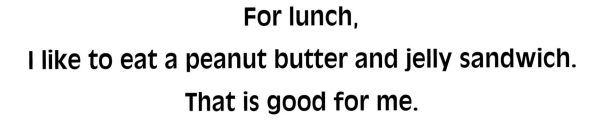

For breakfast,
I like to eat toast and jelly.
That is good for me.

For lunch,
I like to eat a peanut butter and jelly sandwich.
That is good for me.

For dinner,
I like to eat rolls with butter and jelly.
That is good for me.

All day long,
I like to eat good food.
But best of all, I like jelly!
I like jelly any time!

Shared Reading 7
What Is Good For Me?

Areas of Study
Language Arts, Health, Science

Title of Shared Reading
What Is Good For Me?
By Cinda Moon

Text Structure
Narrative Story

Primary Purpose
To provide practice for students on monitoring known words

To introduce students to a narrative and repetitive form of text

To introduce students to a study of nutrition and healthy habits

Lessons
First Reading Focus:
To Develop Understanding

- Predict what this text will be about, based on the title and the illustrations.

- Question the students about healthy habits.

- Read the text and encourage a discussion about foods that are healthy and good for you. Ask the students to compare their predictions to what the text actually says. Discuss how making predictions based on our knowledge of a subject matter helps us understand what we read.

- Discuss favorite foods. Have the students decide if jelly is good to eat at every meal.

- Reread the text several times while providing opportunities for discussion.

Additional Readings:
To Develop Strategies and Skills

Strategies
- While rereading with the students, use a pointer to show correct matching of voice to words. Point out two-syllable words, such as *peanut, butter, jelly, breakfast, any,* and *dinner.* Clap the syllables and look at the spaces between the words. Instruct the students about word boundaries and what a word is.

- After rereading, have the students find known words in the text. You may choose to highlight high frequency words such as, *for, like, to, that, me,* and *is.* Discuss how known words help readers monitor and know that what they have read is correct.

Skills
- Reread the text and discuss how punctuation marks influence the way we read. Locate the periods. Encourage the students to discover that periods are not at the end of each line, and that our reading voice must not stop until we get to a period.

- Reread the text and identify other punctuation marks.

Future Readings:
Other Possible Teaching Points
- Locate and chart words that have long vowel sounds (*like, eat, toast, me, peanut, rolls, day,* and *time*) and short vowel sounds (*jelly, that, lunch, butter, sandwich, dinner, long,* and *best*).

- Sort words by syllables and interactively write a chart of one-syllable and two-syllable words.

Classroom Extensions
- Create a student-generated list of favorite foods and write the foods on sentence strips. Add a small picture for additional support. Write the frame, I like to eat _____ on sentence strips. Place them in a pocket chart to make an interactive reading center.

- Graph the students' favorite foods.

Additional Resources
Hoban, R. *Bread and Jam for Frances.* HarperCollins Books, 1986. ISBN 0064430960

Lord, J. *The Giant Jam Sandwich.* Houghton Mifflin Company, 1972. ISBN 0395442370

Westcott, N. *Peanut Butter and Jelly (A Play Rhyme).* Dutton Children's Books, 1987. ISBN 0140548521

Happy Talk

When we talk to people, our words can make them feel happy or sad. Some words that make people feel happy are:

"Hi!"

"Please."

"Thank you."

"Will you play with me?"

"You did a great job."

"Are you okay?"

"Can I help you?"

"You look nice today!"

"Happy birthday!"

"I'm sorry."

Can you use some words to make people happy today?

Shared Reading 8
Happy Talk

Areas of Study
Language Arts, Social Studies

Title of Shared Reading
Happy Talk
By Marie Belt

Text Structure
List

Primary Purpose
To establish a community of learners in the classroom that emphasizes friendship and mutual respect

To help students learn appropriate language

Lessons
First Reading Focus:
To Develop Understanding
- Read the title and ask the students to predict what "happy talk" might be.

- Read the first two sentences before the list. Ask the students to respond with suggestions of words that make them feel happy. Read the list and check for similar words already included.

- Read the whole text, emphasizing the idea that it is important to use words that make others feel happy and not sad, and that at school the students will be expected to use those kinds of words.

Additional Readings:
To Develop Strategies and Skills

Strategies
- Use puppets to act out different scenarios that allow the students to use words from the text. Encourage them to verbalize different appropriate expressions.

- Reread the text. Discuss how this text is organized. The first and last sentences begin at the left side of the page and continue until there is no more space on the right side. The list, in the middle, is different. Discuss how we still read from the left to the right and return to the left again at the end of each line in the list.

Skills
- Locate all the capital letters in the text. Discuss when it is appropriate to use a capital letter.

- Reread the text. Point out the question marks, periods, and exclamation points and discuss how punctuation influences the way text is read. Locate the question marks and reread

A related interactive writing about friends.

the text with the students, using correct intonation. On subsequent days, choose other punctuation marks to model fluent reading.

Future Readings:
Other Possible Teaching Points
- Locate words that contain the digraph *th*. Discuss whether the sound comes at the beginning, middle, or end of the word.

- Locate and highlight the quotation marks in the text. Discuss their function in the text.

Classroom Extensions
- Use interactive writing to add to the list in *Happy Talk*.

- Take photos of students in classroom situations that illustrate the expressions in the text. Display the photographs with the text.

Additional Resources
Chapman, C. *Pass the Fritters, Critters.* Simon & Schuster, 1993. ISBN 0153072784

Clements, A. *BIG AL.* Scholastic, Inc., 1988. ISBN 0590444557

Hobie, H. *You Are My Sunshine.* Little, Brown & Company, 1999. ISBN 0316365629

Pfister, M. *The Rainbow Fish.* North-South Books, 1992. ISBN 059048169X

Shaughnessy, D. *Let's Talk About Good Manners.* Rosen Publishing, 1997. ISBN 082395045X

January	
February	
March	
April	
May	
June	
July	
August	
September	
October	
November	
December	

Our birthday graph

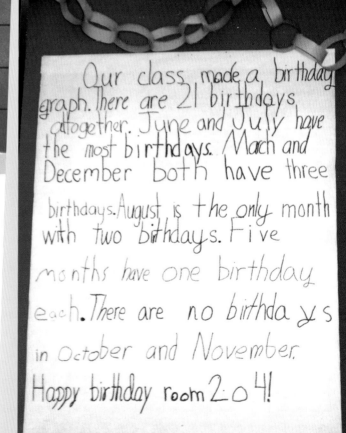

Our class made a birthday graph. There are 21 birthdays altogether. June and July have the most birthdays. March and December both have three birthdays. August is the only month with two birthdays. Five months have one birthday each. There are no birthdays in October and November. Happy birthday room 204!

Shared Reading 9
Happy Birthday!

This shared reading was constructed as an interactive writing where the students and teacher negotiated what to write and then shared the pen to do the writing. This is a good way to make the connection between reading and writing. Interactive Writing and Interactive Editing, a companion book by the same authors, is available from Dominie Press.

Areas of Study
Language Arts, Mathematics

Title of Shared Reading
Happy Birthday!

Note: *The interactive writing that you create in your classroom can be used as shared reading. The lesson that follows is an example of how to use an interactive writing as a shared reading text. You may choose to recreate the same type of interactive writing lesson first and then use it for shared reading with your students.*

Text Structures
Graphic Organizer (Pocket Chart Graph), Expository Paragraph

Primary Purpose
To reinforce the concepts discussed during interactive writing and make connections between the writing and reading processes

To collect personal data about students

To analyze the data collected

Lessons
First Reading Focus:
To Develop Understanding
- After the students and teacher write the months of the year, read and arrange the months chronologically in the pocket chart and graph the students' birthdays. Prompt the students with questions regarding the graph. Ask them:

    How many students do we have in our class?
      How do you know?

    How many students have a birthday in July?

    Which month has the *most* birthdays?

    Which month has the *least* birthdays?

- The students then interactively write an interpretation of the questions discussed and answered about the graph.

- Reread and compare the interactive writing to information from the graph. Reread and compare the interactive writing to information from the graph. Ask the students to question, clarify, and respond to the text.

Additional Readings:
To Develop Strategies and Skills
Strategies
- Reread the text and locate known words in the paragraph. Prompt the students to explain how they knew the words.

- Reread the text and match the months listed in the paragraph to those on the birthday graph. How many months are discussed in the paragraph? Which months are not written about in the paragraph?

Skills
- Reread the text and discuss the order of the months in the pocket chart. Take all the months out and rearrange them in proper order. Try starting with the current month at the top of the chart and proceeding from there. Have the students rearrange the data. Discuss how similar or different the data look.

- Reread the text and highlight the months of the year in the paragraph. Discuss the need for capital letters for all the names of the months.

Future Readings:
Other Possible Teaching Points
- Discuss how 21 could be written, using words. Begin a chart of all the numbers and the corresponding number words.

- Locate math vocabulary in the paragraph: *graph, altogether, most, three, two,* and *one,* and discuss how these words help to analyze the information that was collected.

Classroom Extensions
- Create individual birthday books. Throughout the year, as students have birthdays, each student writes a page for the "birthday student." The pages are compiled in an individual book for the birthday student.

- Collect the birthdates of the siblings of the students in the class and arrange them in a second graph. Discuss the similarities and differences in the two graphs.

Additional Resources
Mora, P. A *Birthday Basket For Tia.* Simon & Schuster Children's Books, 1992. ISBN 0027674002

Murphy, S. *Lemonade For Sale.* HarperCollins, 1997. ISBN 0064467155

Polacco, P. *Some Birthday!* Simon & Schuster Children's Books, 1993. ISBN 0671871706

Whitehead, A. *Tiger Math: Learning to Graph from a Baby Tiger.* Henry Holt Books, 2000. ISBN 0805062483

Yankee Doodle

Yankee Doodle went to town, a-riding on a pony,

Stuck a feather in his cap and called it macaroni.

Yankee Doodle keep it up, Yankee Doodle dandy,

Mind the music and the step and with the girls be handy.

Father and I went down to camp along with Captain Gooding

And there we saw the men and boys, as thick as hasty pudding.

Yankee Doodle keep it up, Yankee Doodle dandy,

Mind the music and the step,

And with the girls be handy.

Shared Reading 10
Yankee Doodle

Areas of Study
Language Arts, Social Studies

Title of Shared Reading
Yankee Doodle

Text Structure
Song

Primary Purpose
To provide students with the opportunity to match oral language with written text

To provide practice with looking at print

To provide practice with monitoring known high frequency words

Lessons
First Reading Focus:
To Develop Understanding

- Have the students become familiar with the selection by singing the song many times without the printed copy available.

- Explain to the students that what is said can also be written down and read. Explain that the words that they have been singing have now been written down and can be read.

- Ask the students to talk about how poems and songs are similar. Read the text with the students.

- Clarify ideas and vocabulary that may be unfamiliar to the students.

Additional Readings:
To Develop Strategies and Skills

Strategies
- Reread the selection and locate known words in the text. Prompt the students to verbalize how they know the words.

- After rereading the text, ask the students to locate and highlight the known high frequency words. Reread and point to each word clearly. Discuss how our voice must match with the text and how the words we know help us to match the words on the page to our voice.

Skills
- Reread the selection and add high frequency words found in the text to the word wall for the students to use as a resource when writing.

- Reread the text and point out the names. Refer to the class name chart and explain that names are always capitalized.

A related interactive writing about George Washington.

Future Readings:
Other Possible Teaching Points

- Reread the text and look at the words, *cap, mind,* and *handy.* Ask the students to think of other words that mean almost the same thing. Talk about how these words make the song more interesting. Choose some common words that the students use frequently in their writing, such as *went.* Begin a list of other words that can be used in place of these words. This list can be used as a resource for the students' writing.

- Reread the text and locate words that that are unfamiliar to the students. Reread the surrounding text. Ask the students to try to figure out the meanings of the words. Use the context, as well as their background knowledge.

Classroom Extensions
- Initiate a study about George Washington.

- Make Yankee Doodle hats for students to wear as they perform the song at a patriotic assembly.

Additional Resources
Kellogg, S. *Yankee Doodle.* Simon & Schuster Books, 1996. ISBN 0689807260

Playhouse Publishing. *Yankee Doodle Dandy.* 2000. ISBN 1571515445

Quackenbush, R. *Pop! Goes the Weasel and Yankee Doodle.* HarperCollins Children's Books, 1988. ISBN 0397322658

Vote

I will vote today.

Let me have my say.

I have read the news.

Now, I may choose.

Win or lose,

A candidate, I must choose.

Yes, this is the day.

I can finally vote my way.

Shared Reading 11
Vote

Areas of Study

Language Arts, Social Studies

Title of Shared Reading

Vote

By Paula J. Jones

Text Structure

Poetry

Primary Purpose

To introduce students to the concept of voting and its purpose in a democratic society

Lessons

First Reading Focus:
To Develop Understanding

- Read the title and have a discussion to determine the students' prior knowledge about voting.

- Predict what the text will be about, based on the discussion.

- Read the text. Clarify words or ideas that are unclear. Ask the students to restate the message in their own words.

- Reread the text several times, providing opportunities for discussion and clarification.

Additional Readings:
To Develop Strategies and Skills

Strategies

- Reread the text. Ask the students how they think the author feels about voting. Ask them to provide examples from the text to support their answers. Discuss how readers use clues from the text to infer what isn't directly stated.

- Reread the text. Highlight the word *candidate* and write it on a Magna Doodle®. Show how long words can be broken into smaller parts. Underline *can*, *did*, and *ate* separately. Demonstrate how to look for and read each part separately, then blend the parts together to read the whole word.

Skills

- Reread the text and highlight *news*, *choose*, and *lose*. Discuss how the same sound is spelled in different ways. Read other familiar shared reading pieces to search for words with similar sounds and spelling patterns. Create lists, sorting the words by spelling patterns.

Future Readings:
Other Possible Teaching Points

- Reread the text and locate words that contain the letter y.

- Reinforce the terms, first and last letter, determine where the y occurs, and sort.

Classroom Extensions

- Allow the students to vote for something, using secret ballots. Tally their votes and record the results.

- Use a class graph to record the results of the voting. Use more than one type of graph to display the same results.

- Create a literacy center in which students compose questions for others to respond to by voting.

Additional Resources

Brown, M. *Arthur Meets the President*. Little, Brown & Company, 1992. ISBN 0316112917

Fradin, D. *New True Books: Voting and Elections*. Children's Press, 1986. ISBN 0516412744

My Garden Spot

I wanted to grow a vegetable,
What do you think I'd need?
I had a little garden spot,
So what I needed was a seed.
First I took my shovel,
And I made a little mound.
Next I took my seed,
And I planted it in the ground.
I watched it and I watered it,
I looked at it every day.
I recorded everything I saw,
And then I went off to play.
I marched out to my garden spot,
And what do you think was there?
Tiny sprouts all colored green!
"Hurray!" I shouted in the air.

Shared Reading 12
My Garden Spot

Areas of Study
Language Arts, Science

Title of Shared Reading
My Garden Spot
By Debra Wakefield

Text Structure
Poetry

Primary Purpose
To introduce students to the steps involved in planting and growing a seed

To work with past tense verb forms

Lessons
First Reading Focus:
To Develop Understanding
- Make predictions, based on the title, about what this text will be about.

- Question the students regarding any unknown vocabulary (*mound, shovel, sprout*), and discuss contextual clues.

Additional Readings:
To Develop Strategies and Skills

Strategies
- Reread the text. Ask the students to think of a physical action that illustrates the action described in the text. Reread the text, using motions.

- Reread the text and ask the students if there are any words that they do not know and that need clarifying. Allow other students to share their understandings. Encourage conversation about definitions and problem-solving strategies.

Skills
- Reread the text and locate words that end with *–ed*. Ask the students to listen to the differences in the sound that *–ed* makes when the words are read aloud.

- Write the *–ed* words on word cards and sort them by similar sound.

- Read the text again, paying attention to the pronunciation of words ending with *–ed*.

- Read other familiar shared reading pieces and look for *–ed* words to decode and add to the word sort.

Future Readings:
Other Possible Teaching Points
- Reread the text and search for synonyms.

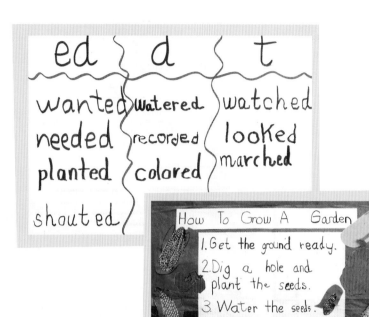

- Reread the text and locate question marks. Discuss how our voice changes when we read questions. Look for other familiar texts that have question marks and read them fluently.

Classroom Extensions
- Plant seeds and record the students' observations as the plants grow.

- Create a literacy center with *–ed* words to sort by sound.

Additional Resources
Ehlert, L. *Growing Vegetable Soup*. Harcourt Brace Jovanovich, 1987. ISBN 0-15-232575-1.

Azarian, M. *A Gardener's Alphabet*. Houghton Mifflin Company, 2000. ISBN 0618033807

Bunting, E. *Flower Garden*. Harcourt, 2000. ISBN 0152023720

Ehlert, L. *Planting a Rainbow*. Harcourt Brace & Company, 1988. ISBN 01526260913

Pattou, E. *Mrs. Sptizer's Garden*. Harcourt, 2001. ISBN 0152019782

Schumaker, W. *In My Garden*. Chronicle Books, 2000. ISBN 0811826899

How to Carve a Pumpkin

Materials Needed
A pumpkin
A knife
A spoon
A marker or crayon
A candle
Some newspaper

Directions
1. Put some newspaper on a table.
2. Put your pumpkin on the newspaper.
3. Cut around the stem to make a lid.
4. Save the lid.
5. Clean the pumpkin. Scrape the insides. Scoop out the seeds.
6. Draw some eyes, a nose, and a mouth on the pumpkin.
7. Cut out the face.
8. Put a candle inside.
9. Put the lid back on the top of the pumpkin.
10. BOO!

Shared Reading 13
How to Carve a Pumpkin

Areas of Study
Language Arts, Social Studies

Title of Shared Reading
How to Carve a Pumpkin
By Marie Belt

Text Structure
Steps in a Procedure

Primary Purpose
To introduce students to nonfiction text that is written in the format of step-by-step directions

To reinforce and practice the concept of return sweep

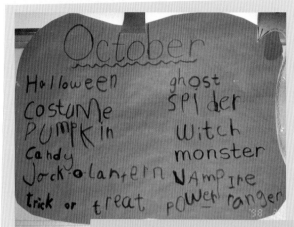

Two Halloween-related interactive writings.

Lessons
First Reading Focus:
To Develop Understanding
- Display the text. Ask the students to notice and comment on the text arrangement.

- Discuss how types of texts are arranged in different ways, depending on the author's purpose.

Additional Readings:
To Develop Strategies and Skills

Strategies
- Reread the text, making sure to point to each word while reading fluently. Refer to step Number 5, which contains two lines of print. Demonstrate reading a sentence that has been broken apart on two lines.

- Prepare pictures to go with the text. As different portions are read, point to the pictures and ask how they relate to the specific step.

Skills
- Write the lines of text on sentence strips, along with a simple picture cue. Place the strips in a pocket chart, out of order. Begin to read the text, allowing the students an opportunity to notice errors. Discuss why the text does not make sense this way. With the students, rearrange the sentence strips in the correct order.

- Locate all the words in the text that begin with the letter s (*spoon, some, stem, scrape, scoop,* and *seeds*). Write the words on individual word cards.

Future Readings:
Other Possible Teaching Points
- Reread the text and choose words that are high frequency and add them to the word wall.

- Compare different text structures by reading the nursery rhyme, "Peter, Peter, Pumpkin Eater."

Classroom Extensions
- Create a literacy center for the students, using a pocket chart and sentence strips. Write directions on strips and have the students put them in order.

- Bake pumpkin seeds and interactively write the step-by-step directions for baking.

Additional Resources
Titherington, J. *Pumpkin, Pumpkin.* Greenwillow Books,1986. ISBN 0688-056954

Cooper, H. *Pumpkin Soup.* Farrar, Straus & Giroux, Inc., 1999. ISBN 03743616490

Hall, Z. *It's Pumpkin Time!* Scholastic, Inc., 1994. ISBN 0590478400

Kroll, S. *The Biggest Pumpkin Ever.* Scholastic, Inc., 1993. ISBN 0590464639

Sloat, T. *Patty's Pumpkin Patch.* G.P. Putnam's Sons, 1999. ISBN 0399230106

A Family

We all have a family. A family is a group of people who love us and help to take care of us. There are many kinds of families. Some families have a mother and a father, and sometimes brothers and sisters. Many of us live only with our mother or father. Some of us have stepparents. Some of us have foster families. Other families have more than one mother or more than one father. Grandmas and grandpas and aunts and uncles and cousins are part of our family, too. Some families are big, and some families are small. Sometimes we don't get along with the people in our family, but we still love them. People in families care about one another.

Shared Reading 14
A Family

Areas of Study
Language Arts, Social Studies

Title of Shared Reading
A Family
By Marie Belt

Text Structure
Expository Paragraph

Primary Purpose
To demonstrate searching for cues

To introduce students to a definition of a family

To introduce students to an expository text structure

Lessons
First Reading Focus:
To Develop Understanding

• Read the title aloud and ask the students to make predictions about the text. Listen and respond to their discussion.

• Read the paragraph aloud. Ask the students to listen for information that was included in previous discussions and for any new information.

• Facilitate further discussion. Ask the students:
   What did the text say that we talked about?
   What did the text say that we didn't talk about?

• Encourage the students to talk about their own families. There may be titles of family members that were not mentioned, such as *abuela* or *tutu*. Emphasize that while all families do not look the same, they have features in common.

Additional Readings:
To Develop Strategies and Skills

Strategies

• With the students, reread the first two sentences of the text. Ask them to think of their initial discussion and predictions about the text. Tell them that this is what readers do as they read for meaning, thinking about what might come next based on what is already known and what has been learned thus far in the reading. Together reread the first two sentences once again and think of family members' names that may appear in the upcoming text. As family titles are named, search for these words in the text and confirm the students' predictions.

• Reread the text, one sentence at a time. Discuss what pictures would illustrate the meaning of each sentence. In pairs, have the students illustrate individual sentences. Reread the text and add pictures. Make the text available for independent reading.

Skills

• Reread the text. Locate words that name family members. Interactively make a list of family names, using words from the text. Add to this list and use it as a resource for reading and writing.

• Locate high frequency words such as *and*, *our*, and *some*.

Future Readings:
Other Possible Teaching Points

• Locate and highlight periods and commas in the text.

• Talk about how punctuation helps us read so that it sounds like talking.

• Read the text with the students several times fluently, stopping and pausing appropriately.

• Use *A Family* to compare and contrast different styles of writing. Use a different text structure (poem, song, or narrative story) to note differences in styles of writing and the reasons authors write for a variety of purposes.

Classroom Extensions

• Interactively write an expository paragraph, using the shared reading as a model to include correct paragraph construction.

• Have the students write about family members independently.

• Paint portraits of family members and display them with the text of *A Family* for independent reading.

Additional Resources
Kuklin, S. *How My Family Lives in America*. Aladdin Paperbacks, 1992. ISBN 0027512398

McBratney, S. *Guess How Much I Love You*. Candlewick Press, 1996. ISBN 076360013X

Ryan, P. *One Hundred Is a Family*. Hyperion Books for Children, 1996. ISBN 078681120X

Tax, M. *FAMILIES*. The Feminist Press at the City University of New York, 1981. ISBN 1558611576

A Season For Everyone

We live on the planet called Earth. The **Earth** is warmed by **heat** from the Sun. During the year, the amount of heat from the Sun changes and causes **seasons**. There are four seasons in a year. The seasons are: **Winter**, **Spring**, **Summer**, and **Fall**. Each season usually lasts about three months. The seasons have different **weather**, **temperatures**, and amount of **daylight**. What is your favorite season?

Season	Months
Winter	December, January, February
Spring	March, April, May
Summer	June, July, August
Fall	September, October, November

Shared Reading 15
A Season For Everyone

Areas of Study
Language Arts, Science

Title of Shared Reading
A Season For Everyone
By Karen Bunnell

Text Structure
Expository Paragraph with Chart

Primary Purpose
To allow students to identify the four seasons and the months in each season

To introduce students to boldfaced words in content area reading

Lessons
First Reading Focus:
To Develop Understanding

- Engage the students in a conversation about how the title may or may not help the reader predict and understand the selection. Ask them if reading the title and making predictions before reading could help us to understand stories read during independent reading. Ask them to think of questions that immediately come to mind after reading the title.

- During the first reading, read one sentence at a time, inviting the students to join in with the reading. After each sentence is read, stop and discuss what was just read.

Additional Readings:
To Develop Strategies and Skills

Strategies
- On additional readings, prompt the students to discuss what to do when you come to a word you do not know in your reading. For example, *The Earth is warmed by _____ from the sun.* How can a strategic reader go about solving this problem? Encourage several responses from the students, illustrating the many ways to figure out the word.

- Reread the text and reinforce strategy prompts: Does it look right? Does it make sense? Can we say it that way? Review some of the questions a reader would ask when reading a new text.

Skills
- Reread the text and discuss the use of boldfaced words.

- Reread the text and count the number of sentences in the passage. Invite the students to the chart to show with a pointer where a sentence starts and where it stops. This is a good opportunity to explain that many sentences start on one line but finish on the next line (reinforce return sweep).

Future Readings:
Other Possible Teaching Points

- The seasons and months of the year in the chart are made to be removable, so on future readings they could be manipulated and rearranged, depending on what month of the year it is.

- As students organize the seasons in the first column, other students are called upon to place the appropriate months next to each season.

Classroom Extensions
- Make individual books, illustrating activities that can be done in each month. The seasons would be included as chapter pages in the book, followed by the three months most often considered part of that particular season.

- The students choose a season (Winter, Spring, Summer, or Fall) and write an acrostic poem, describing the weather or events in that particular season.

Additional Resources
Borden, L. *Caps, Hats, Socks and Mittens: A Book About the Four Seasons.* Scholastic, Inc., 1991. ISBN 0590448722

Gibbons, G. *The Seasons of Arnold's Apple Tree.* Harcourt, Inc., 1991. ISBN 0152712453

Hopkins, L. *Weather: Poems For All Seasons.* HarperCollins Books, 1995. ISBN 0064441911

Iverson, D. *Discover the Seasons.* Dawn Publishers, 1995. ISBN 1883220432.

Addition Mission

Our mission today is to understand **addition**.

If we have five blocks ■ ■ ■ ■ ■ and put

them together with three blocks ■ ■ ■

we can count all the blocks. "1 - 2 - 3 - 4 - 5 - 6 - 7 - 8."

We counted eight blocks **altogether**.

We combined two sets of blocks and

ended up with one total set.

The number 5 can stand for the set of five blocks ■ ■ ■ ■ ■.

The number 3 can stand for the set of three blocks ■ ■ ■.

When we write these numbers on paper

with a **plus sign** in the middle, it looks like this 5 + 3.

We are joining the two sets. This is called **addition**.

An **equal sign** follows the numbers.

We call this an **equation**. 5 + 3 = 8.

We say, "Five plus three equals eight."

Now, your mission is to explain **addition** to a friend.

(Don't forget to bring your blocks!)

Shared Reading 16
Addition Mission

Areas of Study
Language Arts, Mathematics

Title of Shared Reading
Addition Mission
By Karen Bunnell

Text Structure
Expository Paragraph

Primary Purpose
To introduce mathematical vocabulary involved in addition number sentences

To reinforce and review the concept of addition

Lessons
First Reading Focus:
To Develop Understanding

- Discuss the title of the selection. Have the students make predictions. Discuss and clarify terms. Ask them to make predictions about what this piece will be about.

- Read the selection to the students in its entirety. While reading the selection, model with blocks or cubes what the text is explaining. Discuss that they have been doing this in math and this reading piece explains in words the same process.

Additional Readings:
To Develop Strategies and Skills

Strategies

- Reread the text and explain to the students that good readers often make a picture in their mind of whatever they are reading about, like a "video in your brain." Ask them to read along with you and make a picture in their mind about what is read.

Skills

- Reread the text and highlight the mathematical vocabulary: *addition, altogether, plus sign, equal sign,* and *equation.* Clap the syllables in each word.

- Reread the text and locate words that show action: *have, put together, count, combine, write, join, call, say,* and *explain.* Have the students dramatize or demonstrate these actions.

- Reread the text and discuss the use of quotation marks in the passage.

Future Readings:
Other Possible Teaching Points

- On subsequent readings, it is fun to replace the quantity of blocks to form a new equation. The chart shown in the picture has been laminated, and parts of the chart are removable so

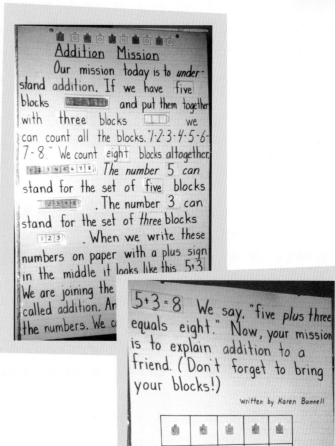

the equation can change. For example, the original problem of 5 + 3 = 8 can be altered to read any number of other combinations: 2 + 3 = 5; 6 + 4 = 10; or 4 + 3 = 7.

Classroom Extensions

- The students could read the chart and demonstrate the joining of sets to another classroom.

- Have the students write their own equations (number sentences) and illustrate each equation with a picture.

- Have the students add the boldfaced words in the selection to a math word bank located somewhere in the room.

Additional Resources

Cato, S. *Addition.* Carolrhoda Books, Inc., 1998. ISBN 1575053209

Long, L. *Domino Addition.* Charlesbridge Publishing, 1996. ISBN 0881068772

Long, L. *Dealing with Addition.* Charlesbridge Publishing, 1998. ISBN 0881062707

Pallotta, J. *The Hershey's Kisses Addition Book.* Scholastic, 2000. ISBN 0439241731

Walton, R. *One More Bunny.* William Morrow & Co., 2000. ISBN 0688168477

Shared Readings

Homophones

Homophones are so confusing to me.
I'm never sure which (or witch) word it should be.
It's hard to know (or no) the word to pick.
I need the right (or write) one to do the trick.

Is a bunny called a hare (or hair)?
If it's not here (or hear) is it over there (or their)?

When it storms, does it pour rain (or rein)?
And does it fall on the window pane (or pain)?

Do we use flour (or flower) to make the bread?
When we finish a book is it read (or red)?

Do I go and buy a new pair (or pear) of pants?
Do I need a special shoe (or shoo) to do a tap dance?

Do we get a tan in the sun (or son)?
When we finish the race first, have we won (or one)?

I'm not sure I know what to do (or dew),
That can really be a help to you (or ewe).
It's a picture in your mind you need to see (or sea),
To let you know which word it should be (or bee).

Shared Reading 17
Homophones

Area of Study
Language Arts

Title of Shared Reading
Homophones
By Debra Wakefield

Text Structure
Poetry

Primary Purpose
To introduce students to the concept of homophones

Lessons
First Reading Focus:
To Develop Understanding
- Read the title of the poem and determine the students' prior knowledge about homophones. If they are unfamiliar with the term, ask them to try to figure out the meaning as they read the poem together.

- Read the text, making sure to use proper inflection. Point to the different homophones while reading to help the students notice the difference.

- Clarify the meaning of the word *homophone* through discussion. Ask the students if they are familiar with any of the homophones used in the poem, and the correct usage.

- Reread the text several times, encouraging the students to read with inflection.

Additional Readings:
To Develop Strategies and Skills
Strategies
- Reread the text. Ask the students to think about what the author is trying to tell the reader about homophones. Ask them to restate the strategy in their own words.

- Reread the text. Point to one of the sentences in which the author is questioning which word to use. Discuss how the author is trying to think through word options and correctly choose the right word. Encourage the students to self-correct in their own reading and writing.

- Examine homophone pairs, focusing on spelling. Help the students see that there are many different ways to spell each sound, and discuss why this is the reason to use more than one source of information when reading. Readers must verify initial visual analysis by checking to see if it also sounds right and makes sense.

Skills
- Locate and record all the homophone pairs that are used in the poem and write them on a chart. Clarify the meaning of each word and ask the students to illustrate each word. Display the chart in the classroom to be used as a resource.

- Reread the text. Return to one of the questions and identify the subject and predicate. Ask the students to use the same words to change the sentence to a statement. Compare the word order in each type of sentence. Talk about the importance of word order and how it affects the meaning of the sentence. Use the same principle to change other questions in the text into statements.

Future Readings:
Other Possible Teaching Points
- Locate the parentheses in *Homophones* and discuss their function in the text.

Classroom Extensions
- Reread familiar shared reading pieces and ask the students to locate homophones.

- Compile the homophones and illustrations into a class resource book.

Additional Resources
Ghigna, C. *See the Yak Yak.* Random House, Inc., 1999. ISBN 0679891358

Gwynne, F. *A Chocolate Moose for Dinner.* Simon & Schuster Children's, 1988. ISBN 0899194354

Ziefert, H. *Night, Knight!* Houghton Mifflin, 1997. ISBN 0395851602

My Mother Says the Strangest Things

My mother says the strangest things that I have ever heard. I
think she forgets I am a child and thinks I am a bird!

When I play with my friends
In the park,
She says, "You're as happy
As a lark."

When I rake up the leaves
From under our big tree,
She says, "You're as busy
As a bee."

When I sit real still
Inside our house,
She says, "You're as quiet
As a mouse."

When I finish my homework
And all is done,
She says, "You're as bright
As the sun."

When I show my courage
Though inside I'm dyin,'
She says, "You're as brave
As a lion."

When I pat her face
With my new mitten,
She says, "You're as soft
As a kitten."

Yes, my mother says the strangest things that I have ever heard.
But my mom is still the greatest, even if what she says is absurd!

Shared Reading 18
My Mother Says the Strangest Things

Area of Study
Language Arts

Title of Shared Reading
My Mother Says the Strangest Things
By Debra Wakefield

Text Structure
Poetry

Primary Purpose
To introduce students to idiomatic expressions

Lessons
First Reading Focus:
To Develop Understanding
- Read the title of the poem and ask the students to make predictions about the text.

- Read the text. Ask the students to check their predictions against the content of the text.

- Discuss how sometimes people use phrases that seemingly do not make sense and we do not understand. These peculiar expressions occur in all languages and are often confusing to those who are unfamiliar with them. Provide some examples and encourage the students to share experiences they have had with such expressions.

- Reread the text and ask the students if they have ever heard any of these expressions.

Additional Readings:
To Develop Strategies and Skills

Strategies
- Reread the text, stanza by stanza, asking the students to clarify the meaning of each expression.

- After meaning has been clarified, ask the students to think of experiences in their own lives that match each expression. For example, *When I play hide-and-seek with my sister, I am as quiet as a mouse.*

- Discuss the text placement on the page. It is arranged in an unusual format. Remind the students that text is read from top to bottom and left to right. We can apply this principle, even when the text is arranged in unusual ways.

Skills
- Locate and highlight words that contain the /er/ sound. Record them on word cards and then sort them according to the spelling.

- Highlight the word *you're*. Discuss the meaning of the word in this poem, and explain that it is a contraction. Compare it to the spelling and meaning of *your*.

- Generate sentences and ask the students to choose the correct word for use in numerous examples.

Future Readings:
Other Possible Teaching Points
- Highlight the idiomatic expressions in the text. Ask the students to compare the expressions, noting likenesses. Emphasize the pattern used, "You're as _____ as a _____." Show the students how this language structure signals the use of an idiomatic expression.

- Locate and highlight all the apostrophes in the text. Discuss the different functions of the apostrophe.

Classroom Extensions
- Read aloud a children's book and listen for examples of idiomatic expressions.

- Interactively write a list of idiomatic expressions and illustrate it to make a class book.

- Create a literacy center that encourages the use of idiomatic expressions. Write expressions on individual sentence strips as a story starter. For example, "I'm as happy as a lark when _____."

- Encourage the students to use idiomatic expressions in their independent writing to make it more interesting.

Additional Resources
Juster, N. *As Silly as Bees Knees, As Busy as Bees: An Astounding Assortment of Similes.* William Morrow & Co., 1998. ISBN 0688163602

Wood, A. *Quick as a Cricket.* Child's Play Ltd, 1982. ISBN 0859533069

Silent Friend

You are my friend.
You depend on me to understand you.

You are my friend.
You have no voice, but I hear you very clearly.

You are my friend.
I can be with you no matter where I am.

You are my friend.
Whether borrowed or bought, you are still my friend.

You are my friend.
You stretch my mind and make me think.

You are my friend.
You keep me company and make me feel better when I am
sad.

You are my friend.
In black and white, or in color, you are still my friend.

Yes, you are my friend.
You never change and that is very rare.

You are my friend.
You are my very special friend.

Shared Reading 19
Silent Friend

A class-inspired riddle.

Area of Study
Language Arts

Title of Shared Reading
Silent Friend
By Paula J. Jones

Text Structure
Riddle

Primary Purpose
To allow students to make inferences, using a topic with which they are familiar

To introduce personification

Lessons
First Reading Focus:
To Develop Understanding
- Read the title and make predictions about the content of the text. Ask the students to think about their predictions as they listen to the text read aloud.

- Reread the text and talk about the ending and how the author did not identify the friend as a book. Discuss who the friend might be. Encourage the students to cite examples from the text that support or deny their ideas. Refrain from telling students the answer. Instead, allow as much time as necessary to sort through the text clues to come to a conclusion.

Additional Readings:
To Develop Strategies and Skills

Strategies
- Reread the text, stanza by stanza. Ask the students to create a picture in their mind that is inspired by the text. Choose key phrases from the riddle for various students to illustrate. Share and compare the different artistic interpretations of the same phrase. Discuss the importance of visualizing pictures in our mind to help us understand text.

- Reread the text. Discuss the varying student interpretations as to who the silent friend is and the reasoning behind them.

Skills
- Reread the text. Locate examples where the author describes the book as if it were a person. Are there other examples of familiar text that the students have read that personify inanimate objects? Discuss the author's purpose for doing this.

- Reread the text. Discuss figurative language as a method used by writers to create more interesting text. Locate examples of figurative language and discuss the idea that the author is trying to express.

Future Readings:
Other Possible Teaching Points
- Define and locate adjectives and adverbs in the text. Talk about the author's word choice and how the words chosen help to make the riddle more interesting and thought-provoking.

- Talk about the structure of a riddle. How does it compare to the other riddles that the students know. List the characteristics of a riddle.

Classroom Extensions
- Interactively write a riddle, using personification and figurative language. Instruct the students to choose words and phrases that are precise and create visual images in the mind of the reader.

- Encourage the students to search for examples of personification in books that they hear read aloud or read independently. Create a class list of books classified this way.

Additional Resources
Bumes, M. *The $1.00 Word Riddle Book.* Addison Wesley Longman, Inc., 1993. ISBN 0941355020

Greene, M. *The Greatest Joke Book Ever: Packed Chock-Full of Japes, Jests, Gewgaws and Gimcracks for Every Occasion...and Then Some!* William Morrow & Co., 1999. ISBN 0689816650

Howe, J. *Bunnicula's Long-Lasting Laugh-Alouds: A Book of Jokes and Riddles to Tickle Your Bunny-Bone.* Simon & Schuster Children's, 1999. ISBN 0689816650

Lyon, G. *BOOK.* DK Publishing, Inc., 1999. ISBN 0789425602

Marzolla, J. *I Spy Gold Challenge: A Book of Picture Riddles,* Scholastic, Inc., 1999. ISBN 0590042963

Weitzman, I. *Joklopedia: The Biggest, Best, Silliest, Dumbest Joke Book Ever.* Workman Publishing Company, Inc., 2000. ISBN 0761112146

I Am Me!
You Are You!

There are so many things to know about me,

Some are like you, I'm sure you'll agree!

Let's share what makes us one of a kind.

Are there things in common you think we'll find?

I like to read books and can write a great story.

Mostly they're nice, but sometimes they're gory.

Pat's a whiz at numbers, he really likes math.

When he's on a roll, don't get in his path.

Sports are one thing that Kim likes to do.

She can do them alone, or with a friend or two.

She's awfully brave, not afraid to take a fall,

She loves softball, soccer, and basketball.

Bill likes school work, and knows it can be fun,

"But, sometimes," he says, "A kid's just got to run!"

He likes to play with his friends, he can never get enough,

"Always behaving yourself can be kind of rough."

I am me, and you are you.

Some things are the same.

Some things are not.

Today is a good day to discover

Just how we are like one another.

So many different things make us who we are,

We can let these differences draw us near or far.

Each thing that we do is just a part,

Finding out about each other is just the start.

Shared Reading 20
I Am Me! You Are You!

Areas of Study
Language Arts, Social Studies

Title of Shared Reading
I Am Me! You Are You!
By Debra Wakefield

Text Structure
Poetry

Primary Purpose
To allow students to understand and appreciate the uniqueness of each individual

To encourage students to identify unique aspects of their own personality

Lessons
First Reading Focus:
To Develop Understanding
- Read the title of the poem aloud and encourage the students to make predictions about the content of the text.

- Read the text. Ask the students to check their predictions against the content of the text.

- Ask the students to think about the things that the children in the text like to do. Ask them to compare the children in the poem to themselves and share their observations about likenesses and differences.

- Reread the poem several times, inviting the students to join in the reading. Encourage pertinent conversations.

Additional Readings:
To Develop Strategies and Skills
Strategies
- Reread the text. Ask the students to find something in the text that relates to them and to share that with the class. Help those who are having trouble making connections to see what they may have in common with the children in the text. Ask the students to draw a picture of themselves to show their connection to the children described in the text.

- Reread the text. Point out how the author gives us many details to help us understand one main theme. Ask the students to talk about what they think the theme of the piece is and to back up their ideas with evidence from the text.

Skills
- Reread the text. Locate and highlight the use of capitalization. Discuss the need for capital letters when writing proper names.

- Reread the text. Ask the students to figure out the main idea of each stanza. Then have them highlight the details the author provides to help develop that main idea.

Future Readings:
Other Possible Teaching Points
- Reread the text and locate the dialogue used in the poem. Note the placement of the quotation marks. Discuss how quotes can be broken in this way, with the speaker inserted in the quotation.

- *Kim*, *Pat*, and *Bill* all contain common rimes. Use these names to create new words, demonstrating on a Magna Doodle® or with magnetic letters.

Classroom Extensions
- Use this poem to help the students learn about one another. Use ideas from the poem to formulate questions they may want to ask one another, such as, "What kinds of things do you like to read?" Develop a list of questions and arrange the students in pairs. Have the students interview one another, using the questions, and report what they find out to their classmates.

- Allow the students to write about themselves, using the questions the class has formulated as a guide. Display their writing accompanied by a self-portrait.

- Encourage the students to write acrostic poetry, using their names and things that make them unique.

Additional Resources
Brandenberg, A. *I Am Me!* Harcourt, 1996. ISBN 0152009744

Kuskin, K. *I Am Me.* Simon & Schuster Children's, 2000. ISBN 0689814739

Carlson, N. *I Like Me.* Pearson Learning, 1990. ISBN 0140508198

Carlson, N. *Making the Team.* Carolrhoda, 1985. ISBN 0876142811

Viorst, J. *Rosie and Michael.* Macmillan Publishing Co., 1974. ISBN 0689712723

A Day in the Life...

The Kitty Chronicles

What a day.

Got up and stretched.

Then took a nap.

Meowed (really quite patiently, I thought),

Until my creature FINALLY got out of bed and escorted
me down to my food dish.

(My bowl was already full, but I don't like to take chances.)

Nibbled a bit.

Curled up in the sun and took a nap.

Woke up and stretched.

Took a nap.

Walked past the window, so THAT DOG could see that I was INSIDE while he was still OUTSIDE.

Laid down in front of the window and took a nap.

Allowed my creature to cuddle and pet me for almost a whole minute. (Anything to make his day.)

Decided to take a rest.

I'm exhausted.

Frisky

Writings from Rover

What a day!

Woke up and ran around the yard about twenty times!

Boy, did that feel good! My blood was pumping!

It was so much fun I ran around twenty more times!

My Master came out to give me some food.

Wow! He is so good to me! I love him SO MUCH!

I barked and jumped and wagged my tail to show him how happy
I was to see him and how much he means to me.

I was SO happy!

He actually stopped and talked to me and petted me and called me a good dog!

WOW! What a great day!

Even THAT CAT didn't bother me, sitting in the house and acting like
she was the queen of the world. (I hate that cat.)

But, MY MASTER loves me! What a great day!

Rover

Shared Reading 21
A Day in the Life...

Area of Study
Language Arts

Title of Shared Reading
A Day in the Life…
By Marie Belt

Text Structure
Narrative Journal Entry

Primary Purpose
To introduce students to the style of personal narrative

To introduce students to the concept of the author's voice being expressed in a piece of writing

Lessons
First Reading Focus:
To Develop Understanding
- Without showing the students the text, read the title aloud: *A Day in the Life…* Ask the students to make predictions about the content of the piece.

- Show the students the entire text, which is displayed in two different fonts. Read the title of each section and ask the students to modify their predictions based on the new information. Discuss the reasons for the modification.

- Read aloud the text of each journal entry, making sure to read with different and distinct voices. Ask the students to comment on what they notice about each entry.

Additional Readings:
To Develop Strategies and Skills

Strategies
- Discuss the placement of the text on the page. Discuss the order in which to read the text; title of the page, and the title and text of individual journal entries. Discuss the concept of top-to-bottom. Relate what students know about reading other text to reading this new format of text.

- Reread the text. Ask the students to talk about the personalities of each writer. Ask them to validate their comments by going back to the text and reading excerpts that support their conclusions.

Skills
- Reread the text, locate and highlight the parentheses and discuss their function. Discuss how the extra comments contained within the parentheses allow the reader to understand more of the character's thoughts.

- Reread the text, locate and highlight different examples of the use of capitals. Discuss the purpose behind the use of

capitalization to create emphasis, as in *SO MUCH*, or to impart meaning about a character's feelings, as in *MY MASTER*.

Future Readings:
Other Possible Teaching Points
- Locate and highlight unfamiliar vocabulary in the text. Ask the students to clarify terms for one another.

- Rewrite the text, deleting the capital letters. Ask the students to read the text and compare its impact with the text that is read with capital letters.

Classroom Extensions
- Divide the class into two sections. Perform a reader's theater with the text, encouraging the students to read with expression and fluency.

- During independent writing, encourage the students to write from another point of view. Use this as a means of beginning a conversation about voice in each student's individual writing.

Additional Resources
Hall, D. & Moser B. *I Am the Dog: I Am the Cat.* Dial Books, 1994. ISBN 0803715048

Harper, I. & Moser B. *My Dog Rosie.* The Blue Sky Press, 1994. ISBN 059047619X

Harper, I. & Moser B. *My Cats, Nick and Nora.* The Blue Sky Press, 1995. ISBN 0590476203

Moss, M. *Amelia's Notebook.* Pleasant Company Publications, 1995. ISBN 1562477846

On Top of Spaghetti

On top of spaghetti,

All covered with cheese,

I lost my poor meatball,

When somebody sneezed.

It rolled off the table,

And on to the floor,

And then my poor meatball,

Rolled out of the door.

It rolled in the garden,

And under a bush,

And then my poor meatball,

Was nothing but mush.

The mush was as tasty,

As tasty could be,

And then the next summer,

It grew into a tree.

The tree was all covered,

All covered with moss,

And on it grew meatballs,

And tomato sauce.

So if you eat spaghetti,

All covered with cheese,

Hold on to your meatball,

Whenever you sneeze.

Shared Reading 22
On Top of Spaghetti

Area of Study
Language Arts

Title of Shared Reading
On Top of Spaghetti

Text Structure
Song

Primary Purpose
To familiarize students with humorous text

Lessons
First Reading Focus:
To Develop Understanding
- Display and read the title of the text for the students. Ask them to make predictions about the content of the text based on the title.
- Have the students become familiar with the selection by singing the text together several times.
- Read the text together. Discuss and clarify ideas and vocabulary as needed.

Additional Readings:
To Develop Strategies and Skills

Strategies
- Reread the text, one stanza at a time. Ask the students to visualize in their minds the actions described in the text. Reread the text again and have the students draw pictures of each stanza that relate to the text. Ask them to share their pictures with the group while rereading the text. Discuss the importance of visualizing pictures in our mind and how this helps readers understand and relate the meaning of the text to their own background knowledge.
- Reread the text for fluency and expression. Authors write text for different purposes. Discuss the humor found in this selection and talk about how the reader expresses the author's purpose through fluent reading.

Skills
- Reread the text. Search for and locate words with long vowels. Highlight words with long vowel sounds. Make word cards with words for students to sort by similar vowel sounds.
- Reread the text and locate words with inflectional endings: *covered, sneezed, rolled,* and *tasty*. Review and discuss the concept of how root words are changed by adding inflectional endings. If necessary, demonstrate on a Magna Doodle® how a common inflectional ending changes a variety of known words.

A student-written definition of compound words.

- Rewrite the text on sentence strips. Pass out the strips to various students and have them line up, putting the sentences in sequence. Read the completed text together and compare it to the written chart for accuracy.

Future Readings:
Other Possible Teaching Points
- Reread the text and locate compound words in order to review this concept.
- Reread the text and discuss how authors get ideas for writing. Use this text to show the students how a common, everyday occurrence can be turned into a humorous piece of writing.

Classroom Extensions
- Look for other songs that are written with the same tune, pattern, and structure. Innovate a text and write a new song.
- Make a big book with illustrations for the students to revisit during independent reading.
- Interactively write other silly songs, using a common text structure and tune.

Additional Resources
Prelutsky, J. *The New Kid on the Block.* Greenwillow Books, 1990. ISBN 0688022715

Prelutsky, J. *A Pizza the Size of the Sun.* Greenwillow Books, 1996. ISBN 0688132359

Sierra, J. *Monster Goose.* Harcourt, Inc., 2001. ISBN 0152020349

The Pledge of Allegiance

I pledge allegiance to the flag

of the United States of America

and to the Republic for which it stands,

one nation under God, indivisible,

with liberty and justice for all.

Shared Reading 23
The Pledge of Allegiance

Area of Study
Language Arts

Title of Shared Reading
The Pledge of Allegiance

Text Structure
Pledge

Primary Purpose
To allow students to discuss their understanding of a piece of familiar text

To encourage patriotism by developing deeper understanding of a familiar text

Lessons
First Reading Focus:
To Develop Understanding

- Have the students become familiar with the selection by reciting the text many times without the printed copy available.

- Introduce the text by having the students read the title and asking them what they know about The Pledge of Allegiance. Ask them to share their experiences with reciting the Pledge, as well as their understanding of the text.

Additional Readings:
To Develop Strategies and Skills

Strategies
- Reread the text, phrase by phrase. Ask the students to restate the meaning of each phrase in their own words. Clarify unfamiliar words or concepts, and encourage the students to think of examples from their own lives that exemplify each idea.

Skills
- Locate words that contain the letter *g*. Separate them according to their sound, either hard *g* or soft *g*. Note the –*dge* spelling pattern at the end of *pledge*. Ask the students to generate other words that end with a soft *g* sound. Record their answers and look for other examples of this spelling pattern.

- Choose key words from the text. Ask the students to restate the meanings of those words, using their own language.

Future Readings:
Other Possible Teaching Points
- Locate the words in the text that are capitalized. Discuss the reasons for the capitalization in each instance.

The Pledge defined in "kid-talk."

- This text has been recited by the children for many years. It should be read with appropriate phrasing. Ask them to compare their phrasing to the punctuation that is represented in the text. Talk about how punctuation and natural language patterns contribute to fluent reading of text.

Classroom Extensions
- Use interactive writing to rewrite the Pledge in "kid talk." Display this text alongside the standard Pledge of Allegiance.

- Ask students who have friends or relatives who are new citizens to come in to share their feelings and experiences when taking the Pledge as a citizen of the United States of America.

Additional Resources
Michelson, Bettie. *We Salute the Stars and Stripes: A Children's Book That Puts Meaning into the Pledge of Allegiance to Our Flag.* 2001. ISBN 0970943601

Munoz-Ryan, P. *The Flag We Love.* Charlesbridge Publishing, 2000. ISBN 0881068446

Martin Luther King, Jr.

Martin Luther King, Jr. was one of the greatest American leaders of the 20th century. He was born during a time when African American people were treated unjustly. In many parts of the United States, people of color were not allowed to vote. They were also not allowed to use the same schools, public water fountains, or swimming pools as white Americans. Dr. King dedicated his life to changing laws that discriminated against people because of their race.

Timeline of Major Civil Rights Events in Martin Luther King, Jr.'s Lifetime

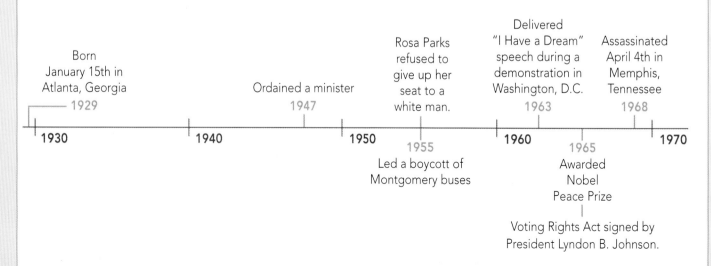

Born January 15th in Atlanta, Georgia 1929

Ordained a minister 1947

Rosa Parks refused to give up her seat to a white man.

Led a boycott of Montgomery buses 1955

Delivered "I Have a Dream" speech during a demonstration in Washington, D.C. 1963

Awarded Nobel Peace Prize 1965

Voting Rights Act signed by President Lyndon B. Johnson.

Assassinated April 4th in Memphis, Tennessee 1968

1930   1940   1950   1960   1970

Grades 23

Shared Reading 24
Martin Luther King, Jr.

Areas of Study
Language Arts, Social Studies

Title of Shared Reading
Martin Luther King, Jr.
By Marie Belt

Text Structures
Expository Paragraph, Timeline

Primary Purpose
To introduce students to the historical figure Martin Luther King, Jr.

To introduce students to a paragraph format

To introduce students to text that is organized, using the structure of a timeline.

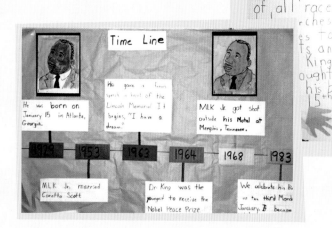

Lessons
First Reading Focus:
To Develop Understanding

- Read the title of the text. Ask the students to share anything they know about Martin Luther King, Jr.

- Read the text of the paragraph. Then read the text of the timeline, pointing to each section as it is read aloud. Talk about the purpose of the timeline and how it is designed to help the reader understand a sequence of events.

Additional Readings:
To Develop Strategies and Skills

Strategies
- Reread each portion of the text. Point out the differences in the way the two types of text are read. Point out the importance of reading the timeline from left to right, regardless of the placement of text around the timeline (either above or below the line).

- Reread the paragraph and highlight significant events mentioned in the text. Then read the timeline and search for those same events. Notice that some, but not all, of those events are represented on the timeline. Note the events represented on the timeline that are not mentioned in the paragraph. Talk about how and why the author chooses items to place on the timeline.

Skills
- Reread the paragraph. Remind the students that paragraphs are groups of sentences that focus on one topic. Compare these sentences to the phrases that make up the text of the timeline. On different days, change the phrases in the timeline to sentences, and the sentences in the paragraph to phrases.

- Reread the text and locate the topic sentence, supporting sentences, and concluding sentence. Highlight and label the parts of the paragraph.

Future Readings:
Other Possible Teaching Points
- Locate examples of events in the timeline that are not recorded in the paragraph. Interactively write timeline phrases into detailed sentences and insert them into the paragraph.

- Locate and highlight transitional words that help the author show the passage of time.

Classroom Extensions
- Look for examples of timelines in other texts. Compare the types of information that can be recorded.

- Use interactive writing to create a class timeline to display information for a content area the class is studying.

Additional Resources
Adler, D. *A Picture Book of Martin Luther King, Jr.* Holiday House, Inc., 1991. ISBN 0823408477

King, M. *I Have a Dream.* Scholastic Press, 1991. ISBN 0590205161

Levine, E. *If You Lived at the Time of Martin Luther King.* Scholastic, Inc., 1990. ISBN 059042582X

Marzollo J. *Happy Birthday, Martin Luther King.* Scholastic Inc., 1993. ISBN 05904400667

No-Calorie Cooperation

Ingredients:

    3 cups respect   1 1/2 cups sharing

    1 teaspoon "I messages"   2 tablespoons creative thinking

    1/2 teaspoon appreciation   1 teaspoon kindness

    3/4 cup listening to others   Positive comments (as needed)

Mix respect, "I messages," and appreciation. Blend listening to others, sharing, creative thinking, and kindness until light and fluffy. Gradually stir in respect mixture. Mix until smooth and well-combined.

Form cooperative groups and wrap mixture in waxed paper. Refrigerate mixture for several hours. Review required tasks and remove mixture from the refrigerator.

Preheat oven to 375° F. Divide the duties among the members of the group by rolling out the mixture one part at a time, 1/2 inch thick. Make sure all have access to the mixture, then sprinkle with positive comments. Flour heart cookie cutters and use to cut out from the mixture.

Bake for 7 to 10 minutes, or until lightly golden. Decorate with good manners.

SERVES ABOUT 3 DOZEN.

Grades
2-3

Shared Reading 25
No-Calorie Cooperation

Areas of Study
Language Arts, Mathematics, Social Studies

Title of Shared Reading
No-Calorie Cooperation
By Karen Bunnell

Text Structure
Recipe

Primary Purpose
To build understanding of the necessary components when working in cooperative groups

To reinforce for students how to read and follow a recipe

Lessons
First Reading Focus:
To Develop Understanding

- Discuss with the students why it is important to cooperate with others.

- Explain that this recipe will describe the necessary ingredients for cooperating with others. Check that the students have the background knowledge of what a recipe is used for, what ingredients are, and how to bake cookies.

- Read the title and ingredients together. Clarify unknown vocabulary and terms.

- Discuss why the chosen ingredients are an important component to this recipe. Are these common ingredients found in real recipes? Connect the ingredients to the students' responsibilities when working in cooperative groups.

- Reread the quantities and ingredients and have the students measure the appropriate amounts, using a bag of flour, a mixing bowl, and measuring utensils.

- Read the steps to complete the recipe and discuss whether this is something we can actually make, or will we be visualizing the steps and imagining that we are making cookies.

Additional Readings:
To Develop Strategies and Skills

Strategies
- Reread the text and ask the students to summarize each direction in their own words. Work in cooperative groups to chart the summary to share with the class. Discuss how the summarizing helped in comprehending the text.

- Compare and contrast this recipe with other recipes. Discuss how this text structure is organized and why. Does this type of organization help the cook to know what is needed and how to complete the task?

Skills
- Reread the text, locate the verbs, and list them. Interactively write the definition for a verb.

- Reread the text and locate the root words that have added prefixes and suffixes. Review and chart the different prefixes and suffixes to use as a resource.

Future Readings:
Other Possible Teaching Points

- Have the students work in cooperative groups to compile a list of additional traits that are important when working with others. Read the lists together.

- Reflect on the recipe ingredients and write independently about the most important ingredient and why it is the most important one.

Classroom Extensions
- Interactively write another recipe.

- Recalculate the quantity of each ingredient needed to serve the entire number of students at your grade level.

Additional Resources:
Bass, J. *Cooking with Herb, the Vegetarian Dragon (A Cookbook for Kids)*. Barefoot Books, 1999. ISBN 184148041X

Better Homes and Gardens Books, *New Junior Cookbook*. Meredith Books, 1997. ISBN 0696207087

D'Amico, J. *The Math Chef*. John Wiley & Sons, Inc., 1997. ISBN 0471138134

Mayer, M. *The Mother Goose Cookbook*. Morrow Junior Books, 1998. ISBN 0688152422

Warshaw, H. *The Sleepover Cookbook*. Sterling Publishing Co., Inc., 2000. ISBN 0806944978

Watson, N. *The Little Pigs' First Cookbook*. Little, Brown and Company, 1987. ISBN 0316924679

Seashells

From Marine Life for Young Readers

A special sac holds the **organs**.
The sac is covered by the shell.
The shell is their home.

◄ Scallop

Seashells are soft animals. They live in hard shells. Their shells protect their bodies.

There are more than 100,000 kinds of seashells. They are members of the mollusk family. Seashells live in the water.

Seashells come in many sizes. Some seashells are gigantic. Some are less than one inch long.

Seashells have tentacles. Each tentacle has one eye. The eye can see in many directions.

Key Content Words	Mr. Swartz's Second Grade Class Interactive Editing Paraphrase
soft hard shells protect	Seashells are soft, so they have hard shells to protect themselves.
100,000 kinds mollusk water	There are over 100,000 kinds of seashells. They are mollusks that live in the water.
sizes gigantic one inch	They are many sizes. Some are gigantic, while others are one inch.
tentacles eye many directions	Seashells have one eye on each tentacle that helps them see in many directions.

Shared Reading 26
Seashells

Area of Study
Language Arts

Title of Shared Reading
Seashells
By Philip Swartz and his Second Grade Class at Garfield
Elementary School, Montebello (California) Unified School District

Text Structure
Expository Paragraph

Primary Purpose
To introduce interactive editing and show how it can be used to analyze and rewrite text

To review sentence structure

To introduce paragraph structure

To introduce seashells as part of a thematic unit on marine life

Lessons
First Reading Focus:
To Develop Understanding

- First read *Seashells* as a read aloud. The reading should be interactive, with the students participating, asking questions, and sharing experiences.

- Discuss new vocabulary.

- This book might be best used as the beginning of a thematic unit on marine life.

Additional Readings:
To Develop Strategies and Skills

Strategies
- Identify the key content words and main ideas in the text.

- Discussions should include which words are important for the key content and which words are secondary in the text.

- Discuss good sentence and paragraph structure.

- Analyze the text to help the students build comprehension through key content words. Use these words to construct a new paragraph, which will be part of a shared reading piece.

Skills
- Reread each sentence. Discuss how a good sentence is constructed, using a subject and predicate.

- Reread the text. Discuss the importance of topic sentences, supporting sentences, and concluding sentences.

- Ask the students questions about the final product. These might include:
    Has the original meaning of the text been altered?
    Was the text improved through our work?
    What other changes could be made?

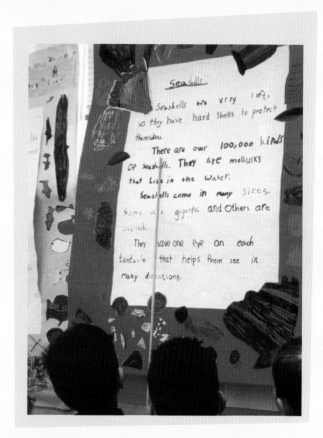

Future Readings:
Other Possible Teaching Points
- Use the key content words to write alternative sentences and discuss how these words might change the meaning of the text.

- Have the students construct multiple-choice questions where the key content words are the answers.

Classroom Extensions
- Use the key content words in the students' independent writing. Have them write similar passages in their journals and come back as a whole class to discuss which words were picked and why.

- This can be done in a similar format as interactive editing, where one day the students find the key content words, and on another day they construct new sentences. On yet another day they can form an introduction and concluding sentences.

Additional Resources
Arthur, A. *Shell: Eyewitness Books*. Dorling Kindersley, 2000. ISBN 0789458306

Swartz, S., Klein, A., & Shook, R. *Interactive Writing and Interactive Editing*. Dominie Press, Inc. 2001. ISBN 0768505348

Swartz, S., & Yin, R. *Seashells*. Dominie Press, Inc., 1999. ISBN 0768503558

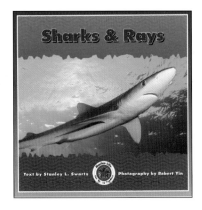

December 19, 2001

Dear Dr. Swartz and Mr. Yin,

Our class has been learning about the ocean. We really like your books about all the different sea creatures. Our favorite book is Sharks and Rays because of all the great shark facts and underwater photos. We took a survey in our class, and sharks are our favorite sea creature.

How did you learn so much about sharks? We have been reading lots of shark books and are trying to become shark experts. How did you take all those pictures of the sharks? Were you in a shark cage, or did you swim with the sharks? Were you scared when you took the pictures? We learned that shark teeth are razor sharp.

We hope you answer our letter. Please write more books about sharks.

From,

Mrs. Parker's
Third Grade Class

Sharks and People

Most sharks are not dangerous to people. The **diver** in this picture is able to get close to this shark.

◄— Diver with Nurse Shark

Shared Reading 27
Letter to Dr. Swartz and Mr. Yin

Areas of Study
Language Arts, Science

Title of Shared Reading:
Letter to Dr. Swartz and Mr. Yin
By Marie Belt

Text Structure
Friendly Letter

Primary Purpose
To provide students with a model of the friendly letter format

To discuss the need to consider your audience when writing a text

To provide an example of writing for an authentic purpose

Lessons
First Reading Focus:
To Develop Understanding
- Read aloud several books from the *Marine Life for Young Readers* series from Dominie Press as a part of a unit of study on the ocean or as an introduction to nonfiction texts.

- Display the shared reading text. Ask the students to look at the format of the text and describe it.

- Read the text of the letter to the students. Ask them to compare their predictions with the actual content.

Additional Readings:
To Develop Strategies and Skills
Strategies
- Reread the text. As you do so, use the think aloud technique to help the students make connections to the author of the text. Ask the students to compare themselves to the authors of the letter, noting likenesses and differences.

- Reread the text. As you read, highlight the questions that are listed in the text. Remind the students that good readers ask themselves questions as they read to help themselves understand what they are reading. Tell them that some of their questions will be answered in the text, while others will not. Identify the questions in the letter as examples of questions that were not answered in the text the students had read. Use this discussion to talk about the different ways we can find answers to some of our unanswered questions.

Skills
- Discuss the proper format for a friendly letter. Note and define each part of the letter, as well as its correct placement on the page. You may choose to label the different parts, using interactive writing.

- Look at the content of the letter. Ask the students what the body of the letter includes. In this case, the authors tell the recipients of the letter several things, and end by asking questions that will encourage the recipients to answer the letter. Discuss the fact that letters often follow this organizational pattern.

Future Readings:
Other Possible Teaching Points
- Discuss the use and spelling of abbreviations of titles, such as *Dr.* Ask the students to identify other titles and their abbreviations. List these, using interactive writing. Talk about the fact that these titles are part of a person's name, and that they are capitalized because of this.

- There are many examples of words that contain *r*-controlled vowels. Locate these and list them on word cards. Later, sort these by similar sound or spelling pattern. Note instances of different spelling patterns for the same sound (for example, *survey*, *expert*, and *third*). Using interactive writing, begin a list of words containing the *r*-controlled vowels.

Classroom Extensions
- Use interactive writing to write a friendly letter to a favorite author, photographer, or public figure. Follow the format of the shared reading piece. Send the letter and wait for a response.

- Create a letter-writing center in your classroom.

Additional Resources
Cole, J. *The Magic School Bus on the Ocean Floor*. Scholastic, Inc., 1994. ISBN 0590414313

Berger, M. *Chomp! A Book About Sharks*. Scholastic, Inc., 1999. ISBN 0590522981

Griff, *Shark-Mad Stanley!* Hyperion Press, 2000. ISBN 0786805943

Swartz, S., & Yin, R. *Sharks and Rays*. Dominie Press, Inc., 1999. ISBN 0768503574

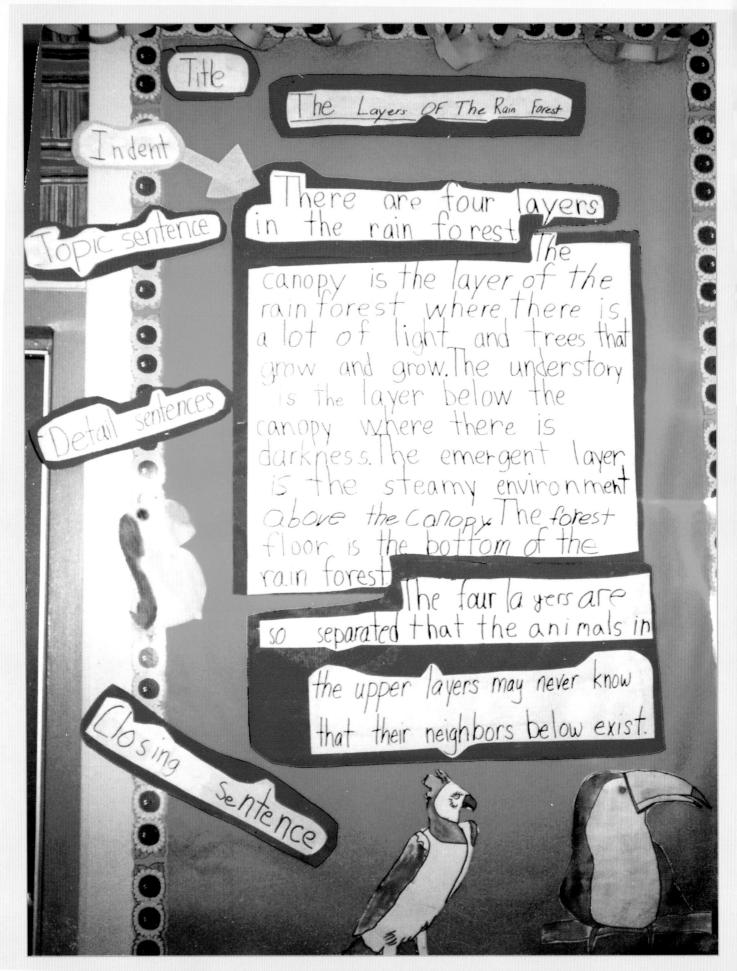

Title

The Layers Of The Rain Forest

Indent

Topic sentence

There are four layers in the rain forest. The canopy is the layer of the rain forest where there is a lot of light, and trees that grow and grow. The understory is the layer below the canopy where there is darkness. The emergent layer is the steamy environment above the canopy. The forest floor is the bottom of the rain forest.

Detail sentences

The four layers are so separated that the animals in the upper layers may never know that their neighbors below exist.

Closing sentence

Grades 2-3

Shared Reading 28
The Layers of the Rainforest

Areas of Study
Language Arts, Science

Title of Shared Reading
The Layers of the Rainforest

Note: The interactive writing that you create in your classroom can be used as shared reading. The lesson that follows is an example of how to use an interactive writing as a shared reading text. You may choose to recreate the same type of interactive writing lesson first, and then use it for shared reading with your students.

Text Structure
Expository Paragraph

Primary Purpose
To reinforce the concepts discussed during interactive writing and make connections between the writing and reading processes

To introduce students to the organization of a paragraph

To review information studied in a content area

Lessons
First Reading Focus:
To Develop Understanding

- The students would have read and reread this selection many times during the written construction of the piece.

- Reread this piece first by reading the labels and then the corresponding phrase or sentence(s). Lead a discussion on whether the labels properly correspond with the text. Ask the students:

    Explain in your own words what a *title, indenting, topic sentence, detail sentences* and *closing sentence* are. In other words, if someone walked into the room and could not read, how would you explain the organization of this paragraph?

    Why do good paragraphs follow this particular format?

    How does organizing the information you know into a concise paragraph help the reader of the text?

Additional Readings:
To Develop Strategies and Skills

Strategies
- Reread the text and discuss the importance of being able to understand what you write as well as what you read. This text introduces students to an organizational structure that enhances comprehension and teaches a writing strategy. Talk

about how this strategy should be used in the students' individual, independent writing.

- Reread the text and discuss how restating facts and details in a paragraph helps clarify and organize the ideas we have learned.

Skills
- Reread the text and review the content vocabulary in the selection. Highlight key vocabulary used in the paragraph (*layers, canopy, understory, emergent layer, environment, forest floor, separated,* and *exist*). Add these to the content area word bank in the classroom.

- Reread the text and discuss the different sounds final y has in words. Point out the following words in the selection for discussion: *canopy, understory,* and *steamy*.

Future Readings:
Other Possible Teaching Points
- Arrange the class into four groups that correspond with the layers in the rainforest. Have each group use the organization learned with this paragraph to construct a paragraph on the assigned layer. Have the students chart paragraphs for other students to label and read.

- Discuss other details that the students know about the layers that were not included in the paragraph. Lead a discussion on how to decide which details to include in a paragraph and which ones to delete.

Classroom Extensions
- Have the students make native rainforest animals, using watercolors to decorate the piece.

- Have them keep a journal for one week in which they describe their trip to the rainforest.

- Turn the classroom into a rainforest, complete with the four layers of the rainforest. Have the students use their creativity to devise the materials for each layer.

Additional Resources
Lasky, K. *The Most Beautiful Roof in the World: Exploring the Rainforest Canopy.* Harcourt, 1997. ISBN 01552008934

Lewington, A. *Antonio's Rainforest.* Lerner Publishing, 1996. ISBN 0876149921

Ross, K. *Crafts for Kids Who Are Wild About the Rainforest.* Millbrook Press, 1997. ISBN 0761302778

Yolen, J. *Welcome to the Greenhouse.* Putnam Publishing, 1993. ISBN 0399223355

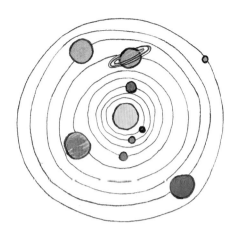

Our Solar System

Our solar system is in the Milky Way Galaxy. There are millions of other systems in this galaxy. The Milky Way Galaxy is part of the universe.

Our Earth is one of nine known planets that go around our star, the Sun. Other objects go around the Sun, too–large chunks of rocks that are called asteroids, balls of ice called comets, and dust particles.

All of the planets move in two ways. Every planet turns around like a spinning top. This movement is called rotating. As each planet rotates, it also follows a path around the Sun. This path is called an orbit. Some planets orbit closer to the Sun than others.

The planets that are closer to the Sun are called the inner planets. They are Mercury, Venus, Earth, and Mars. They all have a hard, rocky surface.

The five planets that are further from the Sun are Jupiter, Saturn, Uranus, Neptune, and Pluto. They are also very far from each other. Their surfaces are not solid, but are probably slushy. Pluto is not like any of the other planets. Pluto is a mystery.

Shared Reading 29
Our Solar System

Areas of Study
Language Arts, Science

Title of Shared Reading:
Our Solar System
By Charlene Huntley

Text Structure
Expository Essay

Primary Purpose
To introduce the students to the format of reading paragraphs of expository text

To help the students understand the movement of the planets in our solar system

Lessons
First Reading Focus:
To Develop Understanding
- Prepare the following list of words from the text: *solar, system, galaxy, universe, planets, movement, rotate*, and *orbit*. Read the words and ask the students to predict the content of the text. Discuss their predictions and explain how background knowledge helped in making the predictions. Discuss why these particular words were chosen.

- Read the first paragraph and discuss any clarifying questions. Discuss predictions based on new information from this paragraph. Are there predictions that need to be revised?

- Repeat these steps with each paragraph.

- Discuss the purpose of this text. Why would the author write this text? Why would a reader choose to read this text? Why is it important to know about this topic?

Additional Readings:
To Develop Strategies and Skills
Strategies
- Reread the text and ask questions that can be answered, using the text as a resource.

- With a partner, identify one or two important words that represent each paragraph. Share the words and discuss how they relate to the main ideas and the title of the text.

- Discuss what a new paragraph signals to the reader. How does the organization of the essay help the reader understand the content?

Skills
- Reread the text and highlight all the nouns and proper nouns. Sort the nouns into categories and interactively write a definition for common and proper nouns. Display the definitions as a resource for future use.

- Reread the text and locate and highlight all the words that begin with a capital letter. Review the rules of capitalization.

Future Readings:
Other Possible Teaching Points
- Interactively write multiple-choice test questions, using this shared reading text as a resource.

- Ask the students what the word *this* means in the second sentence of the third paragraph. Repeat this exercise with other pronouns in the text and discuss pronoun use.

Classroom Extensions
- Draw a model of the solar system and label the planets.

- Write an explanation of how planets move for someone who has never heard of a solar system.

- Write multiple-choice questions for a quiz bowl.

Additional Resources
Bampton, C., and Hawcock, D. *The Solar System*. Readers Digest Children's Publishing, Inc., 1999. ISBN 1575842831

Cole, J. *The Magic School Bus: Lost in the Solar System*. Scholastic, Inc., 1988. ISBN 0590414291

Langen, A., and Droop C. *FELIX Explores Planet Earth*. Abbeville Publishing Group, 1996. ISBN 0789203200

Mitton, J. *Discovering the Planets*. Eagle Books Limited, 1981. ISBN 0816721319

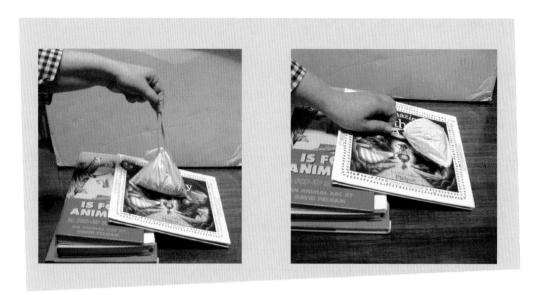

How an Incline Plane Makes Things Easier

Simple machines come in many different styles and are our everyday tools and gadgets. Simple machines can do many things that make our lives easier. They help reduce the amount of energy needed to do a job. An important type of simple machine is the incline plane.

To show how a simple machine makes a job easier, you will need these materials:
1. Four books
2. Ruler
3. Bag of marbles
4. Rubber band

Once you have the materials together, follow the directions below:
1. Stack three books on top of one another.
2. Lean the fourth book against the other three, forming an incline.
3. Tie the rubber band to the top of the bag of marbles.
4. Pick the bag of marbles up in the air and measure how far the rubber band stretches.
5. Drag the bag of marbles up the incline plane until it is at the top.
6. Measure how far the rubber band is stretched.
7. Compare the measurements.

The rubber band stretches less on the incline plane because less energy is needed to move the bag of marbles. Using a simple machine makes the job easier.

Shared Reading 30
How an Incline Plane Makes Things Easier

Areas of Study
Language Arts, Science

Title of Shared Reading
How an Incline Plane Makes Things Easier
By Cathleen Geraghty

Text Structure
Steps in a Procedure

Primary Purpose
To introduce the students to expository text that provides steps to be followed

To introduce the students to one type of simple machine

To allow the students to read a piece of text and then use the information contained in the text to perform a procedure

Lessons
First Reading Focus:
To Develop Understanding
- Read the title of the piece and ask the students to make predictions, based on their background knowledge.

- Read the first section of the text, which explains simple machines. Ask the students to compare their initial predictions with the actual content of the text. Based on the text they have read so far, ask them to predict what the next portion of text will be about.

- Read the rest of the text. Ask the students to check their predictions again. Explain that good readers make predictions both before and during their reading.

- Tell the students they will read the text and follow the steps given to create an incline plane. Read and gather the materials needed. Follow the procedures described in the text. Connect the experience with the final portion of text, which explains the outcome of the procedure.

Additional Readings:
To Develop Strategies and Skills
Strategies
- Reread the text. Highlight the sections that tell about the materials needed and the steps to be followed. Ask the students to visualize each of the materials and steps, and then to work together to create illustrations to accompany the text.

- Reread text. Ask the students to look for words that they do not know or may not understand. Explain that good readers notice and pay attention to words that they do not know, so that they can better understand what they are reading.

- Clarify the meaning of the words that the students were unsure of or did not know. Encourage them to share their definitions of words before you offer an explanation.

Skills
- Discuss the format of the text and the use of numbers to show sequential order. Talk about how the way the text is organized helps us to follow the steps and to keep our place while reading and following directions.

- Reread the text, looking for unusual and interesting words that the author used. Discuss how these words make the text more interesting to read and help create pictures in the reader's mind.

Future Readings:
Other Possible Teaching Points
- Reread, locate, and highlight the colons used in the text. Discuss their function.

- Reread and have students look for examples of *r*-controlled vowels. Write these on word cards and sort them, first according to sound and then according to spelling pattern.

Classroom Extensions
- Ask the students to think about the use of marbles in the example. Ask them to predict whether changing the bag of marbles to a bag of pretzels would change the experience. List the students' predictions and listen to their reasoning. Perform the procedure, using the new materials, and discuss the results.

- Create other simple machines. Use interactive writing to list materials and procedures.

- Ask the students to look for and bring in examples of simple machines to share. Label and create a display.

Additional Resources
Scholastic Books. *Exploring Energy: Power from the Sun, Muscles, Fuel, Machines, Inventions and Atoms*. Scholastic, Inc., 1995. ISBN 0590476408

Strasshofer, C. *Work & Simple Machines*. Frank Schafer Publications, Inc., 1997. ISBN 0764704079

Weiss, H. *Machines and How They Work*. Thomas Y. Crowell Publishers, 1983. ISBN 069004299X

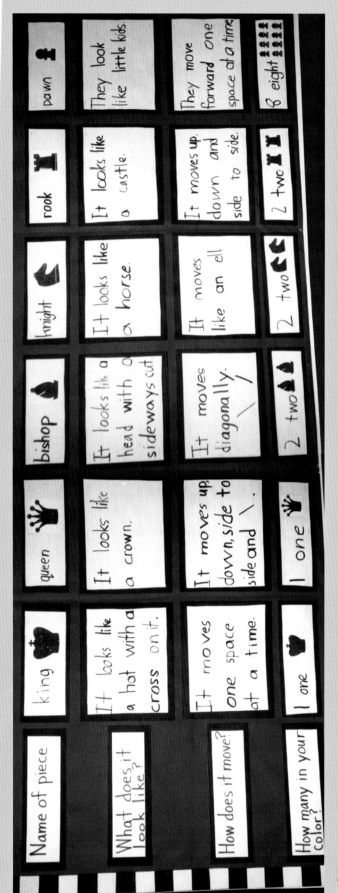

Name of piece	king	queen	bishop	knight	rook	pawn
What does it look like?	It looks like a hat with a cross on it.	It looks like a crown.	It looks like a head with a sideways cut.	It looks like a horse.	It looks like a castle.	They look like little kids.
How does it move?	It moves one space at a time.	It moves up, down, side to side and \.	It moves diagonally. / \	It moves like an ell.	It moves up, down and side to side.	They move forward one space at a time.
How many in your color?	1 one	1 one	2 two	2 two	2 two	8 eight

Chess Interactive Writing

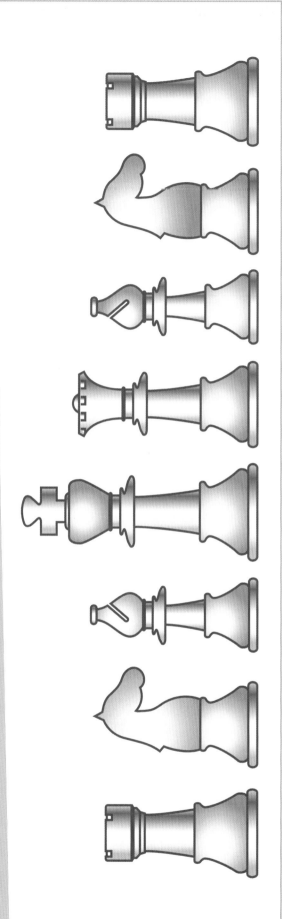

Grades 2-3

Shared Reading 31
Chess Board

Areas of Study
Language Arts, Mathematics

Title of Shared Reading
Chess Interactive Writing

Note: The interactive writing that you create in your classroom can be used as shared reading. The lesson that follows is an example of how to use an interactive writing as a shared reading text. You may choose to recreate the same type of interactive writing lesson first, and then use it for shared reading with your students.

Text Structure
Chart

Primary Purpose
To reinforce the concepts discussed during interactive writing and make connections between the writing and reading processes

To review with the students the use of a chart as a way to organize information

Lessons
First Reading Focus:
To Develop Understanding

- Tell the students they will be reviewing and reading the text they have already organized and interactively written about chess. Review the discussion that determined the decision to write the information in the chart format.

- Review the headings on the chart. Discuss the best way to read the text so that it will make sense to the reader.

- Read the chart, using the manner determined by the students. Talk about whether the method chosen made the text easy or difficult to understand.

Additional Readings:
To Develop Strategies and Skills

Strategies
- Reread the text. Clarify any misunderstandings about text organization or content. Use actual chess pieces to illustrate each section of the chart.

- Review the initial discussion the students had regarding the best way to read the text. Discuss how text can be organized in many ways to help readers understand complicated information. Ask the students to think about what the text would be like if it were organized in a paragraph format. Tell

the students that they must look at information organized in chart formats and decide on the best way to read text so that it makes the most sense.

Skills
- Reread the text and demonstrate the purpose of using the text structure of charting by asking questions about the chess pieces and helping the students find the answer quickly.

- Reread the text and locate examples of questions and answers. Ask a question and allow the students to read the corresponding answer. Then read a statement and ask the students to locate the corresponding question.

Future Readings:
Other Possible Teaching Points
- Reread familiar shared reading pieces that show information organized in different types of charts. Discuss the similarities and differences.

Classroom Extensions
- Shrink the interactive writing text and provide each student with a copy. Arrange to teach another class of students how to play chess, using this chart as a resource. Each student will have one buddy to teach. After the experience, ask the students to reflect on the usefulness of the chart and whether it helped them to effectively teach their buddy about chess.

- Ask the students to look for everyday examples of charts and share them.

Additional Resources
Kidder, H. *The Kids' Book of Chess*. Workman Publishing Company, Inc., 1990. ISBN 0894807676

Lankford, M. *Dominoes Around the World*. Morrow Junior Books, 1998. ISBN 0688140521

Lankford, M. *Jacks Around the World*. Morrow Junior Books, 1996. ISBN 0688137083

MacDonald, D. *Chess For Kids!* Adams Media Corporation, 1997. ISBN 1558507922

Markle, S. *Discovering GRAPH Secrets*. Atheneum Books for Young Readers, 1997. ISBN 0-689-31942-8

We'll Be Making a Prediction

(Sung to the tune of "She'll Be Comin' 'Round the Mountain")

We'll be making a prediction in math class, **Oh yes!**
We'll be making a prediction in math class, **Oh yes!**
We'll be making a prediction,
We call it estimation,
We'll be making a prediction in math class.

Our teacher fills a jar with some things, **Ding-a-ling!**
Our teacher fills a jar with some things, **Ding-a-ling!**
We'll have to think strategically,
To make an educated guess,
She'll ask how we figured it out.

When we all have our prediction written down, **Oh yes!**
When we all have our prediction written down, **Oh yes!**
Now's the time to realize,
How mathematicians visualize,
Can this estimation be utilized?

We estimate every day, **Hey, hey!**
In cooking, banking, and shopping, **Hey, hey!**
I would venture to say,
That estimation pays,
Did you make your estimation today?

Oh, wow, it's awesome to estimate, **Oh yes!**
Oh, wow, it's awesome to estimate, **Oh yes!**
I can totally relate,
And not even hesitate,
The task to really think and estimate.
E S T I M A T E!!

Shared Reading 32
We'll be Making a Prediction

Areas of Study
Language Arts, Mathematics

Title of Shared Reading
We'll Be Making a Prediction
By Karen Bunnell

Text Structure
Song

Primary Purpose
To demonstrate the real-life use of estimation

To review with the students the use of rhythm and rhyme in songs

Lessons
First Reading Focus:
To Develop Understanding
• Introduce the selection by explaining that it has the same rhythm and tune as the song "She'll Be Comin' 'Round the Mountain."

• Sing the first stanza with the students.

• Discuss vocabulary that may be unknown or unfamiliar to the students, and clarify the terms *prediction* and *estimation*.

• Discuss how sometimes authors use phrases that we may not fully understand. Discuss the meaning of the phrase "think strategically to make an educated guess."

• Continue in the same manner through all five stanzas, taking time to clarify and explain words and phrases.

• Discuss how we use the skill of estimation in our daily lives.

Additional Readings:
To Develop Strategies and Skills
Strategies
• Reread the text and locate words that are unknown to the students. Go over strategies that can help them to both decode and discover the meaning of the words they are unsure of.

• Reread the text, modeling pointing to the left side of each line and moving down, line by line, as the print is read. Point out to the students that when they read a text at a rapid pace, their eyes are moving quickly over the lines of print, and that it is difficult to point to each word. Reread the text several times, practicing fluent reading.

Skills
• Reread the text and locate and discuss root words that have suffixes. Highlight each suffix and discuss how it has or hasn't changed the root word.

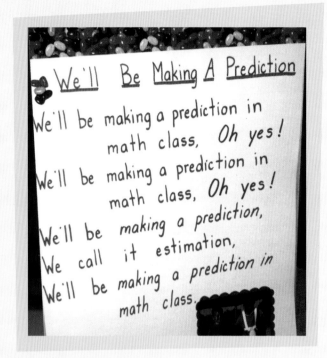

• Reread the piece and locate the multi-syllabic words in the text. Create and arrange the words on a chart, based on the number of syllables in each word. Discuss strategies for using syllables to figure out big words.

• Reread the text and locate the contractions. Review what a contraction is, and discuss the ones found in this text. Create a resource list of contraction words.

Future Readings:
Other Possible Teaching Points
• Connect discussions about estimation and prediction to other content areas.

• Interactively write new words to the tune of "She'll Be Comin' 'Round the Mountain."

Classroom Extension
• Include a weekly estimation jar with a problem. Present the jar and the problem on Monday and allow the students time throughout the week to think and strategize before the solution is revealed on Friday.

Additional Resources
Morgan, R. *In the Next Three Seconds: Predictions for the Millennium*, Vol. 1. Penguin Group, 1999. ISBN 0140566244

Murphy, S. *BETCHA!: Estimating*. HarperCollins Publishing, 1997. ISBN 0064467074

Lee, M. *Estimation Investigations: More Than 65 Activities to Build Mathematical Reasoning and Number Sense*. Scholastic, Inc., 1995. ISBN 0590496026

The Mathematician's Tools

B is for bears, to count in a row,

B is for base ten blocks, we all know.

C is for clocks, to tell me the time,

C is for compass, to draw a curved line.

D is for dominoes, my turn to advance,

D is for dice, to learn about chance.

G is for geoboards, and the bands,

L is for linker cubes, in my hands.

L is for links, to combine end to end,

M is for money, to my friends I lend.

P is for pattern blocks, these I treasure,

R is for rulers, to be sure to measure.

S is for scale, to balance things out,

S is for spinner, "I have no doubt."

T is for tiles, we use every day,

X, is for x-tra cool tools I say,

"Being a mathematician is very okay!"

Shared Reading 33
The Mathematician's Tools

Areas of Study
Language Arts, Mathematics

Title of Shared Reading
The Mathematician's Tools
By Karen Bunnell

Text Structure
Poetry

Primary Purpose
To reinforce initial consonant letters and sounds

To emphasize the purpose of manipulatives when solving mathematical problems

Lessons
First Reading Focus:
To Develop Understanding

- Prepare the text on a chart with a picture of each manipulative adhered to the chart with Velcro®. Assemble real examples of all the manipulatives mentioned in the text.

- Read the title together and discuss the mathematician's job.

- Prompt the students to share the kinds of tools they think a mathematician would use. Allow for discussion, giving the students an opportunity to hear and use new vocabulary.

- Read the text together. Allow the students an opportunity to offer their thoughts about the poem.

Additional Readings:
To Develop Strategies and Skills

Strategies
- Reread the text and search for high frequency words.

- Distribute the real manipulatives to the students. As the poem is reread, the students holding that manipulative will stand up as their tool is being discussed.

Skills
- Locate rhyming words in the piece. Discuss where the rhyming words occur in the text. Discuss how rhyming patterns help the reader when problem-solving new words.

- Explain how knowing a similar word can assist in figuring out a new word by using onset and rime. Demonstrate with words from the text (for example, *advance, chance* helps with *prance, lance, dance*).

Future Readings:
Other Possible Teaching Points

- Locate the commas in the text. Discuss the use of the commas in this text structure.

- Locate and highlight plural words. Discuss adding endings to root words. Use a Magna Doodle® to illustrate *compass* as an example of how to add *–es* as a plural form. Demonstrate other examples of words that end in *s* and how to make them plural.

- Locate the quotation marks and discuss their use.

Classroom Extensions
- Interactively write a class-made chart on how to properly use these tools in the classroom.

- Throughout the year, as manipulatives are introduced and used, compile a chart, listing the various purposes for these tools.

Additional Resources
Borneille, B. *Getting More from Math Manipulatives*. Scholastic, Inc., 1995. ISBN 0590270508

Duffey, B. *The Math Wiz*. Penguin Putnam Books for Young Readers, 1997. ISBN 0140386475

Kenda, M., and Williams, P. *Math Wizardry for Kids: Over 200 Fun & Challenging Puzzles, Games, Designs & Projects for Kids*. Educational Series, Inc., 1995. ISBN 0812018095

Vonderman, C. *How Math Works: 100 Ways Parents & Kids Can Share the Wonders of Mathematics*. Putnam Publishing, 1999. ISBN 0762102330

Back-to-School Shopping

It was that time of the year again. Diane and her mother were ready to go shopping for school supplies at the local department store. Diane carefully folded her dollar bill and put it in her pocket. "I can't wait to go shopping!" she exclaimed.

"Yes, there is a big sale going on right now," replied Diane's mother. "Let's hurry so we can be sure to get the best bargains."

Upon arriving at the store, Diane and her mother quickly found the Back-to-School aisle. "Wow, <u>everything</u> is on sale," Diane shouted.

"Look over there at the big display sign, Diane. It tells us all the sale items and how much each one costs."

Sale
Back-to-School-Supplies

Backpack	65¢	Baseball Cards	15¢
Calculator	44¢	Erasers (6 pack)	10¢
Folder	7¢	Markers (8 pack)	47¢
Notebook (3-ring)	15¢	Pencils (3 pack)	5¢
Ruler	8¢	Scissors	13¢
Supply Box	56¢	Watch	44¢

If you were Diane and had a dollar, what would you buy at the store? How much would you spend, and how much would you have left over?

Grades 2-3

Shared Reading 34
Back-to-School Shopping

Areas of Study
Language Arts, Mathematics

Title of Shared Reading
Back-to-School Shopping
By Karen Bunnell

Text Structure
Narrative Paragraph with Chart

Primary Purpose
To teach problem-solving

To connect mathematics to real-life situations

Lessons
First Reading Focus:
To Develop Understanding

- Read the title and narrative portion of the text together. Stop to discuss or clarify words that may be difficult or unfamiliar to the students. For example: *local, department, dollar bill, exclaimed, replied, bargains, aisle, display sign, items,* and *costs.*

- Explain to the students that the next portion of the piece is an example of a display sign that may be posted in a store. Discuss how to read the chart, the names of the items listed, and the prices.

- Read the chart together, starting with the *Backpack* item and reading down the first column. You should point to each item and price as they are read.

- Conclude by reading the two questions below the supply chart. Ask the students to think about these questions and share with a partner the items they might purchase.

Additional Readings:
To Develop Strategies and Skills

Strategies
- Encourage students to ask questions throughout the reading. During rereading, stop and model out loud the questions you are thinking about as you are reading. Explain to the students that good readers are always asking themselves questions to stay interested in what they are reading.

- Ask the students to answer the two questions at the bottom portion of the text. Encourage them to explain how they decided what to buy and how they know that a dollar would be enough to purchase the items.

Skills
- After the piece has been read many times, encourage the students to begin reading portions of the text in small phrase units. For example, *I can't wait—to go shopping.* Model and demonstrate the use of expression and voice inflection with

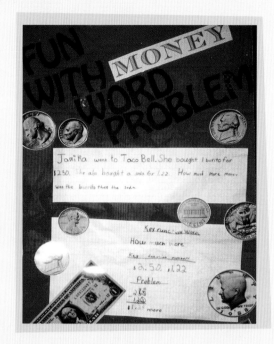

the dialogue section. Invite the students to read along with you to practice expression.

- Discuss and show the start of each paragraph. Talk about indenting a paragraph, especially when a different character begins to speak.

Future Readings:
Other Possible Teaching Points

- Encourage the students to rank the back-to-school supplies, from least expensive to most expensive, and interactively rewrite these items on a separate sheet of paper.

- Revisit and discuss the value of coins and a dollar.

Classroom Extension

- Have the students design their own display sign, using pictures from magazines, with their own writing of the prices. Make display signs available at a literacy center where other students visit.

Additional Resources

Axelrod, A. *Pigs Go to Market: Halloween Fun with Math and Shopping.* Simon & Schuster, 1999. ISBN 0689825536

Bergen, L. *Funny Money.* Price Stern Sloan, Inc., 1999. ISBN 0843178000

Gill, S. and Tobola, D. *The Big Buck Adventure.* Charlesbridge Publishing, 2000. ISBN 0881062944

Wells, R. *Bunny Money.* Penguin Books, 1997. ISBN 0803721463

Williams, R. *The COIN Counting Book.* Charlesbridge Publishing, 2001. ISBN 0881063266

Grades
4-6

Shared Readings

Spelling Right (Rite?)

Bight, bite, byte,

I try with all my might.

To study twenty spelling words,

I need at least one right!

Cent, scent, sent,

It's off to the library I went.

And wrote the words five times each,

Time I felt was so misspent.

Gnu, knew, new,

This list had quite a few.

Oh, memorize each letter's place,

This really stinks, P-U!!

Peak, peek, pique,

I'm studying for a week.

Use each word in a sentence…why?

I want to be a spelling geek!

Right, rite, write,

A story that's out of sight.

"Include each spelling word!"

My teacher will recite.

Way, weigh, whey,

I'm making no headway.

I start to think, not memorize,

A strategy is underway!

Ewe, yew, you,

Can fix spelling miscues.

Think about meanings and patterns,

It all comes into view.

So, when you need to spell,

No yelling, just excel.

Homophones can be real tricky.

There is no magic spell.

Shared Reading 35
Spelling Right (Rite?)

Area of Study
Language Arts

Title of Shared Reading
Spelling Right (Rite?)
By Karen Bunnell

Text Structure
Poetry

Primary Purpose
To develop effective spelling strategies for students

To begin or continue discussion of homophones

Lessons
First Reading Focus:
To Develop Understanding

- Begin a conversation with the students about strategies for being a better speller. Introduce the shared reading text as one student's process to become a better speller.

- Read the entire poem together.

- Reread, stopping to explain any words or ideas the students don't understand.

- Prompt the students to define the three words in each line having the same pronunciation but with different meanings and spellings.

- Ask the students to describe the strategies the student in the poem used to learn to spell.

- Discuss with the students what the author's intent may have been in writing this poem.

Additional Readings:
To Develop Strategies and Skills

Strategies
- Reread the text and discuss the structure used by the author in writing the poem.

- Determine the pattern the poem follows. Discuss how identifying the structure helps to figure out unfamiliar words.

Skills
- Reread the text. Locate and list the homophones. Write a definition of *homophones* and create a homophone word wall. Display the word wall and use it as a resource.

- Reread the text, choose one homophone from each stanza, and interactively write a dictionary definition of that word.

Future Readings:
Other Possible Teaching Points
- Reread the text and interactively chart effective spelling strategies.

- Display the chart as a resource and add to it throughout the year.

Classroom Extensions
- Have the students work in pairs to choose homophones. Use the format of this shared reading piece as a resource for the students to independently write additional stanzas.

- Provide poetry anthologies and books for the students to read independently.

- Ask the students to use the text structure of poetry in their independent writing.

Additional Resources
Dakos, K. *If You're Not Here, Please Raise Your Hand: Poems About School.* Simon & Schuster, 1995. ISBN 0689801165

Frasier, D. *Miss Alaineus (A Vocabulary Disaster).* Harcourt, Inc. 2000. ISBN 0152021639

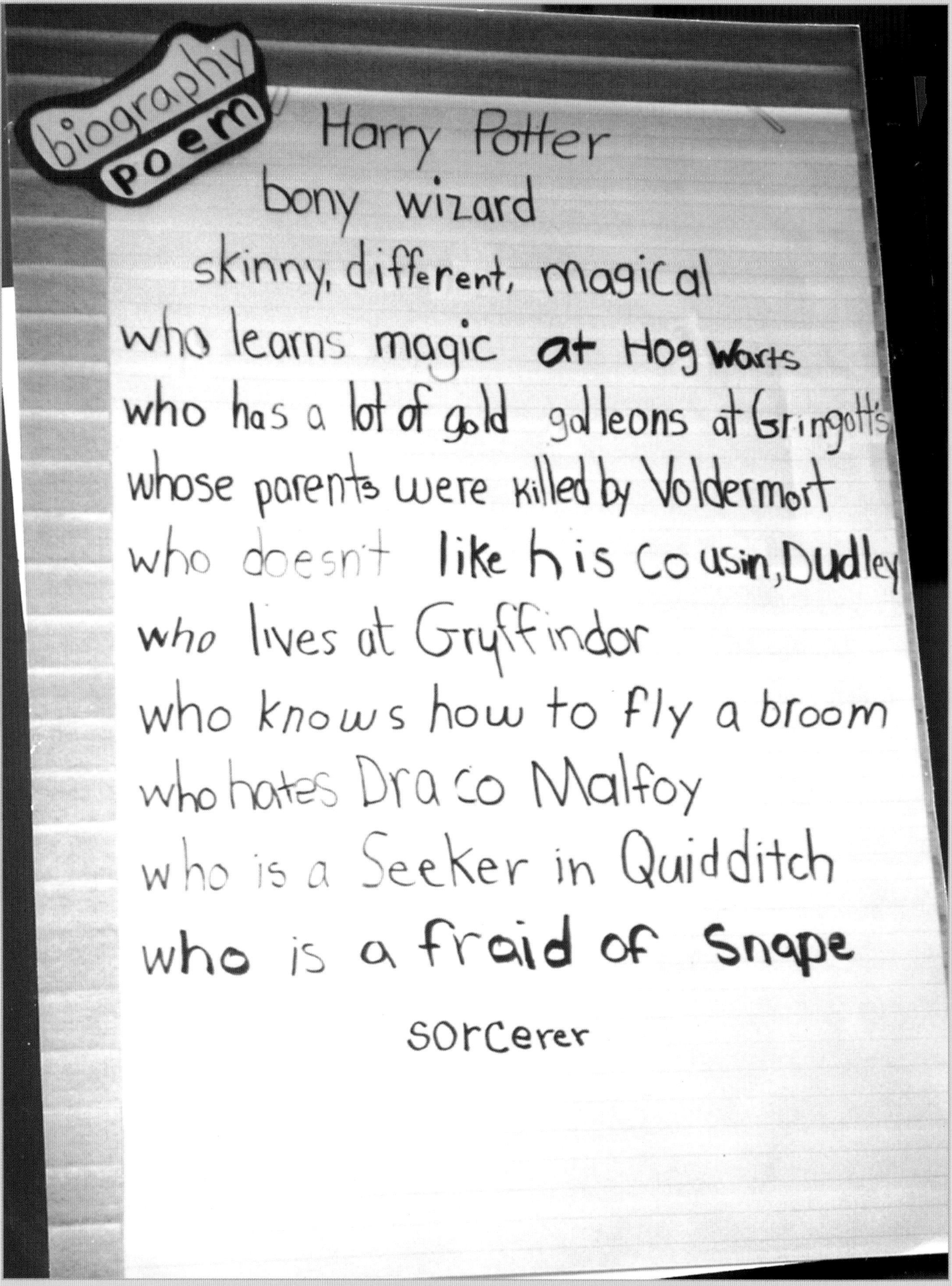

biography
poem

Harry Potter
bony wizard
skinny, different, magical
who learns magic at Hogwarts
who has a lot of gold galleons at Gringott's
whose parents were killed by Voldermort
who doesn't like his cousin, Dudley
who lives at Gryffindor
who knows how to fly a broom
who hates Draco Malfoy
who is a Seeker in Quidditch
who is afraid of Snape

sorcerer

Shared Reading 36
Harry Potter

Area of Study
Language Arts

Title of Shared Reading
Harry Potter

Note: The interactive writing that you create in your classroom can be used as shared reading. The lesson that follows is an example of an interactive writing as a shared reading text. You may choose to recreate the same type of interactive writing lesson first, and then use it for shared reading with your students.

Text Structure
Poetry

Primary Purpose
To reinforce the concepts discussed during interactive writing and make connections between the writing and reading processes

To introduce the students to a poetry text structure

To introduce the students to a biography

Lessons
First Reading Focus:
To Develop Understanding
- This piece was used to creatively compile information learned from reading the first Harry Potter book as a class read aloud.

- Discuss poetry as a text structure. Ask the students:

   Have you ever read or written poetry?

   How is poetry similar to, or different than, other text structures?

   What are some common features you have noticed about poetry? Answers could include: stanzas, white spaces, creative punctuation, phrase units versus complete sentences, can rhyme but doesn't have to.

- Examine the biography poem written as a class and identify some of the common characteristics of poetry.

Additional Readings:
To Develop Strategies and Skills
Strategies
- Reread the Harry Potter poem and discuss how an author decides what important information to include in a biography.

- Reread the text and invite the students to justify each line written in the poem with at least two examples from the book. Facilitate a discussion about the importance of identifying evidence that supports ideas.

Skills
- Reread the text and review subject and predicate (verb) agreement. For example, *Harry Potter* (singular) *learns* (plural) *magic at Hogworts.* Point out the predicates in the poem.

- Reread the text and review *r*-controlled vowels (*ar, er, or, ur* as in *wizard, different, Voldemort, Gryffindor, seeker,* and *sorcerer*).

- Reread the text and review the difference between adjectives (*bony, skinny, different,* and *magical*) and nouns (*wizard, sorcerer, Quidditch, cousin,* and *galleons*).

Future Readings:
Other Possible Teaching Points
- The students can rewrite the selection, using factual, yet different, biographical information based on the most recent version read.

- Compile a word bank of interesting adjectives used in the biography poem, and add additional adjectives to the bank when appropriate.

- Discuss how this construction of a biography poem can serve as a template for future group or individual biography poems.

Classroom Extensions
- Have the students interview a classmate and write a biography poem, using the interactively written example as a template.

- Have them write an autobiography poem about themselves.

- Have the students write an acrostic poem for Harry Potter, using their own name.

Additional Resources
Rowling, J.K. *Harry Potter and the Sorcerer's Stone (Book 1).* Scholastic, 1999. ISBN 059035342X

Rowling J.K. *Harry Potter and the Chamber of Secrets (Book 2).* Mass Market, Paperbacks, 2000. ISBN 0439064872

Rowling, J.K. *Harry Potter and the Prisoner of Azkaban (Book 3).* Scholastic, 1999. ISBN 0439136350

Rowling, J.K. *Harry Potter and the Goblet of Fire (Book 4).* Scholastic, 2000. ISBN 0439139597

What Did Delaware, Boys?

What did Delaware, boys?
What did Delaware?
What did Delaware, boys?
What did Delaware?
She wore a brand New Jersey,
She wore a brand New Jersey,
She wore a brand New Jersey,
That's what she did wear.

Why did California?
Why did Cali-phone ya?
Why did California?
Was she all alone?
She phoned to say, "Hawaii,"
She phoned to say, " How-ah-yee,"
She phoned to say, "Hawaii,"
That's why she did phone.

Where has Oregon, boys,
Where has Oregon?
If you want Alaska,
I'll-ask-a where she's gone.
What did Mississip, boys,
What did Mississip?
What did Mississip, boys,
Through her pretty lips?
She sipped a Minnesota,

She sipped a Minna-soda,
She sipped a Minna-soda,
That's what she did sip.
How did Wiscon-sin, boys?
She stole a New-brass-key,
Too bad that Arkan-sas, boys,
And so did Tennessee.
It made poor Flori-die, boys,
It made poor Flori-die, you see,
She died in Missouri, boys,
She died in Missouri!

Shared Reading 37
What Did Delaware, Boys?

Areas of Study
Language Arts, Social Studies

Title of Shared Reading
What Did Delaware, Boys?

Text Structure
Chant

Primary Purpose
To expose the students to a chant that uses various examples of wordplay in a humorous manner

Lessons
First Reading Focus:
To Develop Understanding

- Display the title of the text and read it aloud for the students. Ask them what they notice about the words in the title, and then make predictions about the content of the text based on those predictions.

- Have the students become familiar with the selection by chanting the text several times together. (Practice the text beforehand, so that you are familiar with correct phrasing and pronunciation.)

- Talk to the students about how the author of this chant played with words in order to create a humorous text, using the names of some of the states. Encourage them to talk about the double meanings of some of the words.

Additional Readings:
To Develop Strategies and Skills

Strategies
- Reread the text. Talk to the students about the fact that texts are written for different purposes. Ask them to talk about this author's purpose (to review the names of some states, and to entertain).

- Go through each stanza of the text. Identify the states that are mentioned. Talk about the pronunciation of the name of each state, and how each sounds like it could refer to other words or phrases. Have the students give the meaning the author intends for each state. Discuss the fact that playing with words in this way is a common method used by humorists. Encourage the students to identify other places they have seen words used in this way (for example, advertisements, jokes, riddles, etc.).

- Encourage the students to work individually or in groups to create comical illustrations of each of the stanzas of the chant. These can be displayed alongside the text.

Skills
- Locate various words the students may not understand. Clarify the meanings with the students.

- Locate the hyphens that are used in the text. Talk about how the author uses hyphens to help the reader pronounce the words in a way that makes the humor more obvious. Explain that the author often uses hyphens in order to clarify meaning.

Future Readings:
Other Possible Teaching Points
- Locate the states that are mentioned in the chant on a map of the United States.

- Look at the names of some of the other states and think about wordplays that might be created using those names.

- Talk about the text structure of this chant. It is written in a question/response format that has a repetitive and predictable pattern. Divide the chant into two parts and have the students read the text in a reader's theater format.

Classroom Extensions
- Use interactive writing to create additional verses to this chant, using the names of other states. Follow the same format, and use similar punctuation to reinforce the meaning and use of those punctuation marks.

- Ask the students to look for examples of other wordplays and to bring these in to share with the class. Encourage them to look in joke books, newspaper headlines, advertisements, cartoons, and television shows. As they bring in the different examples, clarify the humor. (This will especially benefit students who are English language learners.) Create a classroom display of these examples, either in a book or on a bulletin board.

- Encourage the students to write their own wordplays. These may be added to the class display.

Additional Resources
Hopkins, L. *My America: A Poetry Atlas of the United States.* Simon & Schuster Children's, 2000. ISBN 0689812477

Katz, A. *Take Me Out to the Bathtub.* Simon & Schuster Trade, 2001. ISBN 0689829035

Keller, L. *The Scrambled United States of America.* Henry Holt & Company, 1998. ISBN 0805058028

Hoots and Howls Restaurant

Soups and Salads

Eyeball Soup	Sm. 2.99	Lrg. 3.50
Batwing Soup	Sm. 1.99	Lrg. 2.89
Cockroach Noodle Soup	Sm. 3.50	Lrg. 4.25
Caesar Spider Salad		5.99
Tossed Cattail Salad		6.50

Entrees

Worm Spaghetti with Orange Slime		5.59
Mushrooms with Eel Sauce		6.25
Mashed Potatoes with Rat Surprise		7.15
Vampire Burger with Caterpillar Slime		5.95
Roasted Toenails with Blood Sauce		4.75
Crispy Skeleton Burrito		3.99
Hot and Sour Spider Legs	Sm. 3.49	Lrg. 6.50
Grilled Eyeballs Smothered in Blood Sauce		6.87

Desserts

Chocolate-Covered Worm Cookies	1.29
Pumpkin Lizard Pie	2.50
Frog Legs Banana Split	3.39
Werewolf Surprise	.99

Beverages

Chocolate Witches Tea	1.29
Screamy Pepsi-Cola®	1.29
Howling Hot Chocolate	1.29
Scary Serpent Shake	2.99

Grades
4-6

Shared Reading 38
Hoots and Howls Restaurant

Areas of Study
Language Arts, Mathematics

Title of Shared Reading
Hoots and Howls Restaurant
By Karen Bunnell

Text Structure
Menu

Primary Purpose
To practice reading and comprehending a restaurant menu

To integrate reading and mathematical understandings

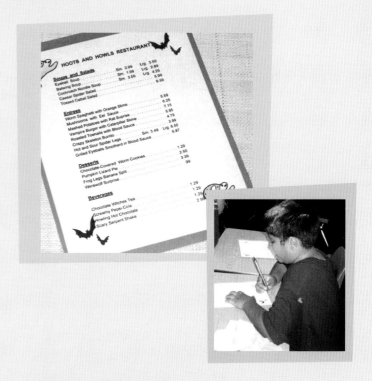

Lessons
First Reading Focus:
To Develop Understanding
- Participate in a discussion about the purpose of menus.

- Begin reading the menu together, starting with the heading of the first food category. After reading the title of each category, ask the students to predict what kind of food they would expect to find under each heading.

- Reread the menu several times, stopping to ask the students what they notice about the way the menu is designed. Clarify their questions and points of confusion.

Additional Readings:
To Develop Strategies and Skills

Strategies
- Reread the text and reinforce how to read the menu. What would readers do if they were only going to have dessert? Discuss the reading of texts organized by headings and how it is not necessary to read sequentially.

- Reinforce the proper reading of the dollars and cents amounts.

Skills
- Reread the text and locate the adjectives on the menu. Change the adjectives and reread the selection.

- Bring in menus from local restaurants. Compare and contrast those menus with the Hoots and Howls Restaurant menu.

- Locate and discuss the abbreviations in the text. List other abbreviations the students are familiar with and discuss the purpose for abbreviations.

Future Readings:
Other Possible Teaching Points
- On repeated readings, orally present the students with a mental math problem. For example: *If I order a small bowl of eyeball soup and screamy Pepsi-Cola®, approximately how much money will I need to purchase this food?*

- Inform the students that there will be a 10 percent reduction in all the prices on the menu. Calculate a few price reductions together and then have the students figure out the prices of the remaining items. Invite them to share their mathematical strategies and calculations with the whole class.

Classroom Extension
- In pairs, have the students create their own menu, using a theme of their choice.

Additional Resources
Horton, J. *Halloween Hoots and Howls.* Henry Holt & Company, Inc., 1999. ISBN 0805058052

Mooerbeek, K. *The Spooky Scrapbook.* Simon & Schuster Publishers, 2000. ISBN 0689834144

Oxenbury, E. *Eating Out.* Penguin Putnam Books for Young Readers, 1994. ISBN 014054948X

Solheim, J. *It's Disgusting and We Ate It! (True Food Facts from Around the World).* Scholastic, Inc., 1998. ISBN 0439133246

A Trek on a Trail

Imagine yourself going on a six-month walk–over prairies, mountains, and deserts. Imagine living with your family and all your possessions in a four-foot by ten-foot wagon that is pulled by two yoke of oxen.

More than 300,000 pioneers did exactly that. Their wagon trains traveled west over the Oregon Trail from the early 1840s through the early 1880s. Those who made the 2,000-mile journey found it an onerous task. Many diaries were written, chronicling their adventure in their wagons, or their "camels of the desert."

Their journals reflect the many difficulties they encountered. For example, falls from animals and wagons, accidental gunshots and illness such as cholera, took many lives. Other threats to their journey's success were storms, floods, mud, dust, snakes, the threat of attacks by Native Americans, and loneliness. As a result of some of these catastrophes, one out of every ten emigrants who started the trip was buried beside the Oregon Trail. In spite of these obstacles, the pioneers forged west with the promise of a fresh start, free land, religious freedom, or gold.

Emigrants started their journey west at Independence, Missouri. Next they passed through present-day Kansas and Nebraska, following rivers where they could get water and find animals for meat. Following the North Platte River, they entered present-day Wyoming near what is now Torrington. At the present-day site of Casper, they followed the Sweetwater River past the landmarks of Devil's Gate, Independence Rock, and Split Rock to South Pass. At South Pass they were able to go up and over the Continental Divide. Next, they came to a place called the "Parting of the Ways," where wagon trains split up going either to Fort Hall or Fort Bridger. After leaving Wyoming, they passed through the present-day states of Utah, Nevada, and Idaho.

Today you can imagine yourself trekking along with an Oregon Trail wagon train. You can experience it by reading accounts of the trip or by actually walking the wagon ruts made by so-called "prairie schooners" many years ago.

Grades 4-6

Shared Reading 39
A Trek on a Trail

Areas of Study
Language Arts, Social Studies

Title of Shared Reading
A Trek on a Trail
By Charlene Huntley

Text Structure
Expository Essay

Primary Purpose
To demonstrate the hardships faced by travelers migrating west in the 1800s

To examine nonfiction text structure

Lessons
First Reading Focus:
To Develop Understanding

- Read the title of the text aloud to the students. With information from the title, combined with their background knowledge, have them generate a list of words that may appear in the text.

- Using the words listed, write a sentence predicting what the shared reading will cover.

- Read the first paragraph and discuss the students' predictions. Revise their predictions, if necessary.

- Continue to read each paragraph, clarifying meaning and referring to the students' predictions.

- Discuss and defend viewpoints about the meaning of the text. Ask the students:

    Does migration always lead to conflict?

    How does geography influence migration?

    How does migration change social, economic, and political orders?

Additional Readings:
To Develop Strategies and Skills

Strategies
- Reread the text and review the strategies readers use to read and understand nonfiction. Ask the students:

    What is the purpose of paragraphs?

    How are nonfiction paragraphs different from narrative paragraphs?

    What is the importance of knowing how different text structures operate?

- Reread the text and summarize each paragraph in one sentence.

- Clarify vocabulary, such as the difference between *immigrant* and *emigrant*. Discuss phrases that cause confusion, such as, *camels of the prairie* and *parting of the ways*.

Skills
- Identify the synonyms in the text and replace them with other choices.

- Review the use of commas.

- Discuss quotation mark use when the text is not dialogue. Look for examples in other familiar texts that show quotation marks used in a similar manner.

Future Readings:
Other Possible Teaching Points
- Discuss the difference between a dash and a hyphen.

- As a class, interactively edit the shared reading text into a newspaper article.

Classroom Extensions
- Using the information from the shared reading, write a first person journal entry that represents a typical day for travelers on the Oregon Trail in the 1800s.

- Identify the common expressions in the text and suggest their possible origins. Discover what these expressions reveal about our culture.

Additional Resources
Erickson, P. *Daily Life in a Covered Wagon.* Puffin Books, 1994. ISBN 0140562125

Loomis, C. *Across AMERICA, I Love You.* Hyperion Books for Children, 2000. ISBN 0786823143

Steedman, S. *A Frontier Fort on the Oregon Trail.* Peter Bedrick Books, 1994. ISBN 0872262642

Van Leeuwen, J. *Going West.* Dial Books for Young Readers, 1992. ISBN 0803710283

Wilson, L. *How I Survived the Oregon Trail: The Journal of Jesse Adams.* Beech Tree Books, 1999. ISBN 0688172768

Career Options

A career is an occupation or profession that people follow throughout their lives. Some people pursue one career, while others choose more than one during their lifetime. Examine the career options below. Which one do you prefer?

Arts
Architect
Dancer
Lawyer
Librarian
Musician
Photographer
Writer

Business Contacts
Bank Officer
Health Service Administrator
Hotel Manager
Insurance Agent
Store Manager
Travel Agent

Business Operations
Accountant
Air Traffic
    Operations
Postal Clerk
Typist
Secretary
Warehouse Worker
Word Processor

Science
Aerospace Engineer
Chemist
Dental Hygienist
Mathematician
Pharmacist
Respiratory Therapist
Veterinarian

Social Services
Corrections Officer
Flight Attendant
Physician
Police Detective
Registered Nurse
Teacher

Technical
Airplane Pilot
Carpenter
Electrician
Firefighter
Maintenance Mechanic
Plumber

Shared Reading 40
Career Options

Areas of Study
Language Arts, Social Studies

Title of Shared Reading
Career Options
By Karen Bunnell

Text Structure
List

Primary Purpose
To discuss how to read and interpret text composed of lists

To expose students to various career options

Lessons
First Reading Focus:
To Develop Understanding

- Ask the students what they have thought about doing when they finish their schooling. Discuss the meaning of the word *career*.

- Together with the students, read the title and the definition at the top of the shared reading selection.

- Prompt the students to think about people they know who have different careers. Entertain many responses from the students.

- Read the boldfaced categories in the shared reading selection. Explain that these are the headings, or categories, that the author used to organize the careers.

- Discuss how to read lists and ask the students which list they would like to read first.

- Read all the careers listed under each category with the students.

Additional Readings:
To Develop Strategies and Skills
Strategies

- Reread the selection to clarify and determine what all vocabulary means.

- Reread the lists in a different order. Discuss whether the order has any bearing on the meaning of the piece. Discuss how recognizing the structure of text helps in accessing the information needed.

Skills

- Reread and locate phonetic elements found in the names of the careers. Concentrate on different skills (consonant blends, final blends, vowel digraphs, and r-controlled vowels) as needed.

Future Readings:
Other Possible Teaching Points

- Add more careers to the list.

- Use this selection as an introduction to further research into careers.

- Have the students choose one career to research. Have them write a paragraph about that career.

Classroom Extension

- Invite various school personnel or local community members into the classroom to share their career choices and knowledge with the students.

Additional Resources
D'Amico, J. *THE MATH CHEF*. John Wiley & Sons, Inc., 1997. ISBN 0471138134

Maze, S. *I Want to Be an Engineer*. Harcourt Brace & Company, 1999. ISBN 0152021094

Maze, S. *I Want to Be a Veterinarian*. Harcourt Brace & Company, 1999. ISBN 0152019650

Guardian of Ancient Secrets

One of the greatest ancient **civilizations** dates back to nearly five thousand years ago, the fourth dynasty of Egypt's Old Kingdom. During this mysterious time, kings known as **pharaohs** were believed to be gods. These early societies glorified the life and death of their pharaohs by building monuments in their honor. One of the most famous monuments is the Great Sphinx of Giza. This Egyptian **sphinx** personifies the body of a lion and the head of a pharaoh. The massive statue is believed to have been carved from a single block of limestone left over in the **quarry** used to build the pyramids. Scholars believe it was sculpted about 4,600 years ago by the Pharaoh Khafe, whose pyramid stands directly behind it. Many **Egyptologists** believe it is Khafe's face that is represented on the Sphinx. Over the years, a large degree of erosion has damaged the original detail of the carved figure, so no one really knows for sure. This marvel has become a symbol of ancient Egyptian culture, representing strength and wisdom, and it continues to mystify **archaeologists** around the world.

Location: Plateau of Giza, Egypt

Date(s) Built: Undetermined

Construction Material: Solid, soft limestone

Weight: Unknown

Total Height: About 66 feet

Total Length: About 240 feet

Paws: About 50 feet long

Head: About 20 feet wide

Shared Reading 41
Guardian of Ancient Secrets

Areas of Study
Language Arts, Social Studies

Title of Shared Reading
Guardian of Ancient Secrets
By Karen Bunnell

Text Structure
Expository Paragraph

Primary Purpose
To teach and reinforce factual information regarding a major archaeological landmark

To clarify content area vocabulary

Lessons
First Reading Focus:
To Develop Understanding

- Read the title of the piece and predict what information the paragraph may include.

- Read the paragraph together. Reread it a second time, pausing after each boldfaced word.

- Participate in a discussion of each boldfaced word. Encourage the students to use their background knowledge, as well as the context of the sentence, to determine the meaning of each word.

- Read the data located below the paragraph together, and discuss the significance of including this information with the paragraph.

Additional Readings:
To Develop Strategies and Skills

Strategies
- Reread the paragraph and clarify unknown or difficult vocabulary.

- Determine new learning or confirmation of previously learned information from having read this piece.

Skills
- Reread the text and highlight all the adjectives. Discuss how their use enhances the overall meaning of the paragraph.

- Reread the paragraph and locate all the prepositional phrases. Review their significance.

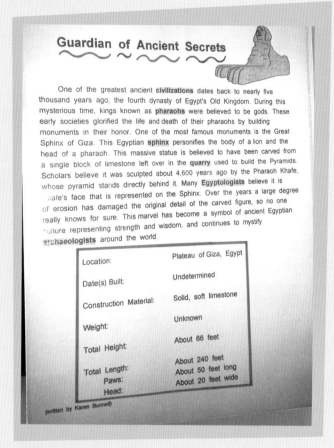

Guardian of Ancient Secrets

One of the greatest ancient **civilizations** dates back to nearly five thousand years ago, the fourth dynasty of Egypt's Old Kingdom. During this mysterious time, kings known as **pharaohs** were believed to be gods. These early societies glorified the life and death of their pharaohs by building monuments in their honor. One of the most famous monuments is the Great Sphinx of Giza. This Egyptian **sphinx** personifies the body of a lion and the head of a pharaoh. This massive statue is believed to have been carved from a single block of limestone left over in the **quarry** used to build the Pyramids. Scholars believe it was sculpted about 4,600 years ago by the Pharaoh Khafe, whose pyramid stands directly behind it. Many **Egyptologists** believe it is Khafe's face that is represented on the Sphinx. Over the years a large degree of erosion has damaged the original detail of the carved figure, so no one really knows for sure. This marvel has become a symbol of ancient Egyptian culture representing strength and wisdom, and continues to mystify **archaeologists** around the world.

Location:	Plateau of Giza, Egypt
Date(s) Built:	Undetermined
Construction Material:	Solid, soft limestone
Weight:	Unknown
Total Height:	About 66 feet
Total Length:	About 240 feet
Paws:	About 50 feet long
Head:	About 20 feet wide

(written by Karen Bunnell)

Future Readings:
Other Possible Teaching Points

- Have the students summarize the paragraph in two or three sentences independently.

- Together as a class, interactively edit the piece, using the students' own words. Include the informational data in the new paragraph.

Classroom Extension

- Have the students research an area of interest related to ancient Egyptian civilization and create their own expository paragraphs.

Additional Resources

Green, R. *Tales of Ancient Egypt*. Viking Penguin, 1996. ISBN 0140367160

Pipe, J. *Mystery History of a Pharaoh's Tomb*. Aladdin Books, Ltd., 1997. ISBN 0761305912

Stanley, D. *Cleopatra*. William Morrow & Co., 1997. ISBN 0688154808

The Mayflower Compact

In November 1620, the Mayflower anchored off Cape Cod, Massachusetts. The Pilgrims had not landed in Northern Virginia as they had planned, and so they were not subject to any European laws. Some people started talking of splitting away from the others, but they were persuaded to stay because it was felt they all had a better chance of survival if they stayed together.

Those who were not members of the Pilgrims worried that the Pilgrim leaders might seize power and force everyone to obey them. They wanted to choose their leaders, just as they chose their pastors in the church. They decided to write down their ideas so everyone could read them and either agree or disagree with them. This became known as the Mayflower Compact, or agreement.

There were 41 men (out of 101 passengers) on board the Mayflower. Only they signed it. Women had few legal rights and so were not asked to sign it, but they were still expected to obey the laws.

The Mayflower Compact established the first form of self-government in the American colonies. In it the signers agreed to join together under one government. They promised to make laws and rules that were fair and would apply equally to everyone, and to obey those laws. This was an entirely new form of rule. Other colonies were forced to obey laws without question. The Pilgrims dared to begin a new method of government. Many years later, it became known as democracy.

Shared Reading 42
The Mayflower Compact

Areas of Study
Language Arts, Social Studies

Title of Shared Reading
The Mayflower Compact
By Sally Keyes

Text Structure
Expository Essay

Primary Purpose
To understand how and why governing bodies and documents are established in a community

Lessons
First Reading Focus:
To Develop Understanding
- Hold a class discussion to help the students build on their background knowledge. Ask them:

   Why do governments limit the freedom of their people?

   How do governments limit the freedom of their people?

   How do communities depend on political systems for structure?

   How do migration and new settlements lead to changes in political order?

- Read the first paragraph of the selection. Solicit and discuss any clarifying questions. Determine if the questions can be answered using the text.

- Have the students work in pairs to summarize the paragraph in one sentence. Share their summary statements with the class.

- Read additional paragraphs in the selection and repeat the above steps.

Additional Readings:
To Develop Strategies and Skills

Strategies
- Reread the text to identify and highlight one or two important words in each sentence. Encourage discussion and reasoning for determining the words. Using the highlighted words and word wall words, interactively write a summary sentence for the shared reading text. Discuss what makes a good summary sentence. Display the sentence and label it as a resource for future reference.

Skills
- Reread the text and locate all the nouns and proper nouns. Divide them into two groups: nouns and proper nouns. Interactively write a definition of each word and display the definitions as a resource for future reference.

- Reread the text and ask the students what the word *it* refers to in the second and third sentences of the third paragraph. Repeat this exercise with other pronouns in the text.

- Reread the text and discuss/review the use of parentheses. Find other familiar texts with parentheses and compare their use.

Future Readings:
Other Possible Teaching Points
- Connect the selection to mathematics by calculating how many Mayflower passengers were men.

Classroom Extensions
- Using highlighted vocabulary words, have the students independently write a paragraph about the need for governing bodies.

- In small groups, using classroom rules and standards, write a class-governing document.

Additional Resources
Lasky, K. *A Journey to the New World: The Diary of Remember Patience Whipple, Mayflower, 1620 (Dear America Series)*. Scholastic, 1996. ISBN 059050214X

Leacock, E., and Buckley, S. *Places in Time: A New Atlas of American History*. Houghton Mifflin, 2001. ISBN 0395979587

Richards, N. *The Story of the Mayflower Compact*. Children's Press, 1991. ISBN 0516446258

Middle Initial Presidents

Have you ever wondered why some United States presidents use their middle initial and others don't? What do those mysterious letters stand for? Here are the fifteen presidents who preferred to use their middle initial and one possible explanation for what each initial stands for (all explanations are based on factual information).

James K. Polk   K for Kibosh
He put a stop to humor, music, and dance at White House parties.

Ulysses S. Grant   S for Scandal
His administration was marked by the first major presidential scandal.

Rutherford B. Hayes   B for Buzz
Give him a "buzz." He was the first president to use the telephone.

James A. Garfield   A for Assassinated
He was shot at the age of 49. Months later, he died of blood poisoning.

Chester A. Arthur   A for Angler
Many people felt he was the best fisherman in America.

William H. Taft   H for Hurl
He was the first president to throw the ceremonial ball to open the baseball season.

Warren G. Harding   G for Ghastly
Widely known as the worst president who was riddled with numerous scandals.

Franklin D. Roosevelt   D for Disabled
At age 39 he was struck with polio, which left his left leg paralyzed.

Harry S Truman   S for Straightforward
This president was known to be honest, almost to a fault.

Dwight D. Eisenhower   D for Dauntless
He was considered the greatest American military hero of World War II.

John F. Kennedy   F for Fortune
He was a millionaire by age 21, and the wealthiest president. He declined the presidential salary, as did George Washington.

Lyndon B. Johnson   B for Belcher
He belched loudly whenever he felt like it, and helped himself to other people's plates.

Richard M. Nixon   M for Malfunction
He was the only president to resign for attempting to cover up criminal acts.

Gerald R. Ford   R for Robust
He was often deemed our most athletic president. He was a football star and was offered two professional team contracts.

George W. Bush   W for We'll See
He was recently elected president, so Americans will have to wait and see what he will accomplish.

Shared Reading 43
Middle Initial Presidents

Areas of Study
Language Arts, Social Studies

Title of Shared Reading
Middle Initial Presidents
By Karen Bunnell

Text Structure
Expository

Primary Purpose
To present factual information about historical figures in a humorous manner

To create interest in the personalities of presidents and highlight their tenure of office

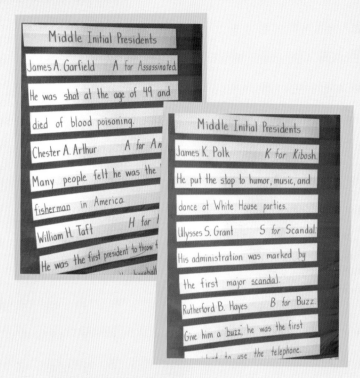

Lessons
First Reading Focus:
To Develop Understanding

- Hold a class discussion to share prior information about specific presidents.

- With the students, read the first five presidents and the explanations for their middle initials.

- Prompt the students to think about whether the information presented is fact or fiction. Discuss how a reader goes about confirming information in a text.

- Continue to read the remaining presidents and the possible explanations for their middle initials.

Additional Readings:
To Develop Strategies and Skills

Strategies
- Reread portions of the text. Discuss the way the text is arranged on the page and the use of capitalization and bold print. These features are signals to the reader that the text is important in some way.

- Reread the text, asking the students to look for words that are unclear to them. Go to the text to try to determine the meaning of the words. Use a dictionary to confirm the meanings.

Skills
- Reread the text and discuss the use of a middle initial rather than the entire middle name. Have the students research what the presidents' initials really stand for and share their findings.

- Based on the information presented in the selection, encourage the students to think of other words that each middle initial could stand for.

Future Readings:
Other Possible Teaching Points

- Create a class presidential character trait word wall, reinforcing positive characteristics of past presidents.

- Encourage the students to research other presidents. Allow them to create their own additions to the list, using information they learn from their research. Compile the list into a class book or display.

Classroom Extensions
- Rewrite the explanations of the presidents' middle initials, using other factual information.

- Allow the students to create a game about the presidents. List several true and one false statement about each president on a game card. The person who draws the game card must decide which piece of information is false.

Additional Resources
Krull, K. *Lives of the Presidents*. Harcourt Brace & Company, 1998. ISBN 015200808X

Nolan, T. *Plays About the Presidents*. Scholastic, Inc., 1996. ISBN 0590481959

Provensen, A. *The Buck Stops Here: The Presidents of the United States*. Harcourt Brace & Company, 1997. ISBN 0152016287

St. George, J. *So You Want to be President?* Philomel Books, 2000. ISBN 0399234071

"No! No! King George…"

"King George, King George,
We must face the facts…
Parliament must raise money!
In our American Colonies,
We must raise the tax."

A series of Acts,
Would soon come to be;
And make their mark on merchants
Throughout each colony.

Sons and Daughters of Liberty
Would now take a stand.
They wouldn't permit
Taxation Without Representation
In their new land.

"Repeal these taxes,
And boycott British goods!"
Colonists would time and again protest.
With goods unsold and taxes unpaid,
Colonists and British relations
Would soon be put to the test.

The failure to tax paper
And end Colonial trade,
Would soon cause the British to stir.
The Colonists' anger and resentment
They could no longer deter…

Propaganda in the newspapers
Would now make history.
As angered Bostonians
Tossed into their harbor,
The precious British East Indian Tea.

The British closed Boston Harbor
With the Intolerable Acts.
But this move backfired,
As more angered Colonists
Refused to pay their tax.

All the trade ended.
The Colonists would unite.
Those things that divided them
Now made them strong.
And for their freedom
They would bravely fight.

Shared Reading 44
"No! No! King George..."

Areas of Study
Language Arts, Social Studies

Title of Shared Reading
"No! No! King George..."
By Peter Burke

Text Structure
Poetry

Primary Purpose
To enhance a unit of study on the Revolutionary War
To review poetry format

Lessons
First Reading Focus:
To Develop Understanding
- Display the title of the poem and read it aloud to the students. Note the quotation marks and ask the students to think about whom this poem might be addressing and what the content might include.

- Display the rest of the text and read it aloud with the students. Ask them to check their initial predictions against the text.

- Reread the text and encourage a discussion that clarifies its meaning.

Additional Readings:
To Develop Strategies and Skills
Strategies
- Reread the text. Choose multi-syllabic words and demonstrate how to decode them by first breaking the word into smaller parts and then using onset and rime patterns.

- Reread the first stanza of the text. Demonstrate the comprehension strategy of questioning by modeling a question the reading has created in your mind. Continue reading through the next stanzas, pausing to model questions and encouraging the students to contribute their own questions.

Skills
- Reread the text and locate words with common prefixes and suffixes. List these words on word cards. Sort the cards and define the meaning of each prefix and suffix. Post the definitions in the classroom as a resource, along with the list of words from the poem.

Future Readings:
Other Possible Teaching Points
- Reread the text and look at the quotes used. Talk about how quotes affect the meaning and strength of a written piece.

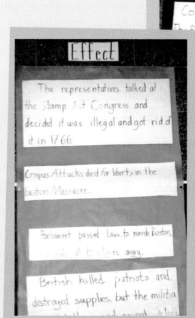

Students wrote the cause and effects of Revolutionary War events.

- Reread each stanza of the text. Locate and highlight key phrases and words that are the most important in understanding the text. Use those key words and phrases to restate the content of the text.

Classroom Extensions
- Create a class mural depicting the events described in the poem. Encourage the students to add appropriate speech bubbles to the mural, using the quotes from the characters in the poem. Display the mural, along with the text, throughout the unit of study.

- Use interactive editing to change the format of the text from a poem to a paragraph or timeline.

Additional Resources
DePaola, T. *Can't You Make Them Behave, King George?* Coward McCann, 1977. ISBN 0698114027

Draper, A. *Boston Tea Party: Angry Colonists Dump British Tea.* Rosen Publishing Co., 2000. ISBN 0823945717

Knight, J. *Sailing to America: Colonists at Sea.* Troll Communications, 1998. ISBN 0816745552

Kroll, S. *The Boston Tea Party.* Holiday House, 1998. ISBN 0823413160

Moss, M. *Emma's Journal.* Harcourt Brace, 1998. ISBN 0152163255

School Memo

DATE: _____ , 20___

TO: _____'s Class

FROM: The Principal's Office

RE: Science Fair

There will be a school Science Fair in four weeks. All classrooms will participate by submitting science projects. Each classroom may decide how to determine the projects, but each project must follow the procedure listed below. Thank you in advance for your hard work.

STEPS TO CREATE A SUCCESSFUL PROJECT

Step One: Title
Choose an interesting title for your project.

Step Two: Problem
Identify the question or what you are trying to find out.

Step Three: Hypothesis
Include an educated guess about what may happen in your experiment.

Step Four: Materials
List everything that was used to conduct the experiment.

Step Five: Procedures
Step by step, list what you did in your experiment.

Step Six: Observations
Compile what you saw by using graphs, pictures, data, etc., and display the observations.

Step Seven: Results
Briefly summarize what you found out from doing your project.

Shared Reading 45
School Memo

Areas of Study
Language Arts, Science

Title of Shared Reading
School Memo
By Karen Bunnell

Text Structure
Memorandum

Primary Purpose
To help the students understand how to read and follow a memorandum

To reinforce the steps of the scientific method

Lessons
First Reading Focus:
To Develop Understanding
- Introduce the word *memorandum* or *memo* to the students. Discuss their prior knowledge or exposure to this particular text structure.
- Read the memo together, stopping to discuss the organization of the information.
- Clarify any unknown words or ideas.
- Reread the memo numerous times to enhance comprehension.

Additional Readings:
To Develop Strategies and Skills
Strategies
- Reread the text and discuss thoroughly the Steps to Create a Successful Project.
- Interactively write the steps to the scientific method on a chart, summarizing each step in the students' own words.

Skills
- Compare and contrast the format and punctuation of a memo to that of a friendly letter.
- Discuss the similarities of a memo and an e-mail message.

Future Readings:
Other Possible Teaching Points
- Conduct science fair projects, using the memorandum as a resource.
- Generate a class list of other topics that might be addressed using a memo.

Classroom Extensions
- Ask the students to choose a partner and begin planning their science project.
- Ask the students to individually write a memo to a person of their choice, following the format used in this shared reading.

Additional Resources
Madgwick, W. *Questions and Answers.* Kingfisher Publications, 2000. ISBN 0876288093

Mandell, M. *Simple Science Fair Projects with Everyday Materials.* Sterling Publishing, 1989. ISBN 0806957646

Moutran, J. *Science Teacher's Almanac.* Center for Applied Research in Education, Professional Publishing, 1992. ISBN 0876288093

Risaclas. F., and Pearce, Q. *My First Science Fair Project.* Lowell House Juvenile, 1997. ISBN 1565657359

Struggle to Freedom

The British wanted to dominate the Earth,
And back in the early 1700s
They tried desperately to increase their worth.

Against the French they would take a stand
And attempt to take control of North America's
Resources and land.

A Seven Years' War would soon take its toll,
On British and French soldiers alike,
Even the Natives would soon play a role.

The Iroquois learned about politics
And called both sides their friend,
But in reality it was neither side
That they would defend.

The war became expensive for Britain,
As they paid their many soldiers a fee.
It was a debt that would soon
Change the course of history.

But the lesson the Colonists learned,
Proved to be more valuable than gold,
"THEIR PRIDE WAS IMMEASURABLE,"
It would later be told.

The Colonists' new army could fight with the best,
And in the Revolutionary War,
The Redcoats would soon
Put them to the test.

Their new army fought fiercely and bravely,
For their dreams were at stake.
Their hard earned wages
The king would no longer take!

Shared Reading 46
Struggle to Freedom

Areas of Study
Language Arts, Social Studies

Title of Shared Reading
Struggle to Freedom
By Peter Burke

Text Structure
Poetry

Primary Purpose
To enhance a unit of study on the events leading up to the Revolutionary War

To examine poetry text structure

Lessons
First Reading Focus:
To Develop Understanding

- Display and read the title of the text. Ask the students to think about the word *struggle* and to try to think of any situations that can be described as a struggle. Clarify the meaning of the word through the discussion.

- Display and read the text of the poem aloud. Ask the students to talk about their understanding of the poem and how it relates to what they have learned so far in their unit of study. Reread a stanza at a time to encourage conversation.

- Reread the text and return to the initial discussion about the word *struggle*. Ask the students to relate their personal struggles to the struggles experienced by the Colonists.

Additional Readings:
To Develop Strategies and Skills

Strategies
- Reread the text. Highlight figures of speech or phrases that may be unfamiliar to the students. Some examples include *take a stand*, *take its toll*, and *the course of history*. Clarify their meaning through discussion.

- Reread each stanza of text. Ask the students to think of situations in their lives, from other texts, or from the news that are similar to the ones described in the text. Tell them that good readers try to make personal connections as they read, and that connections help the reader understand text.

Skills
- Reread the text. Locate and highlight words that use apostrophes to show possession. Discuss the placement of the apostrophe and the reason for the different locations.

- Reread the text and locate adverbs containing the suffix *–ly*. Explain that this ending can be added to many adjectives to create adverbs. Review the function of adverbs in text.

Future Readings:
Other Possible Teaching Points
- Reread the text and locate the homonyms. Clarify their meanings and review alternative spellings and meanings for each one.

- Look for memorable quotes, such as, "Their pride is immeasurable," that epitomize key ideas and feelings from this period of time in history.

Classroom Extensions
- Interactively write text to accompany and expand on the ideas presented in this poem. Provide starters, such as, "The sun never sets on the British Empire," that the students must complete in nonfiction format.

- Invite the students to write additional stanzas to the poem, depicting information that is not represented.

Additional Resources
Hopkins, L. *Hand in Hand: An American History through Poetry*. Simon and Schuster, 1994. ISBN 067173315X

Kirkpatrick, K. *Redcoats and Petticoats*. Holiday House, 1999. ISBN 0823414167

Levy, E. *If You Were There When They Signed the Constitution*. Scholastic, 1987. ISBN 0590451596

Lunn, C. *Charlotte*. Tundra Books, 1998. ISBN 0887763839

Miller, M. *Words That Built a Nation*. Scholastic, 1999. ISBN 059029881X

Munoz-Ryan, P. *The Flag We Love*. Charlesbridge Publishing, 1996. ISBN 0881068454

Scillian, D. A Is for America. Sleeping Bear Press, 2001. ISBN 1585360155

Taking a Bite Out of the BIG APPLE

Up and Away Airlines
Ticketless Travel
Non-Transferable. Positive Identification Required

Receipt and Itinerary
Confirmation Number: BunJxc
Passenger:

Flight #233	Date:
Depart LAX	8:35 A.M.
Arrive JFK	4:45 P.M.
Flight #235	Date:
Depart JFK	12:30 P.M.
Arrive LAX	5:35 P.M.

Daily Itinerary
Destination: New York City, New York

Day 1

Board Up and Away Airlines Flight #233 at 8:35 A.M. Arrive at John F. Kennedy International Airport at 4:45 P.M. Board Carey Airport Express bus and travel to your hotel. After checking into the hotel, enjoy the charming row houses, hidden alleys, and leafy courtyards of Greenwich Village. Walk to a local restaurant for dinner.

Day 2

Ride the subway to Battery Park, located at the southern tip of Manhattan. Board the Circle Line Ferry and travel to the Statue of Liberty in New York Harbor. Upon arrival, climb the 354 steps from the entrance to the crown (highest level open to visitors). Return to the ferry and travel to Ellis Island. Tour the restored museum and retrace steps that nearly 17 million people passed through from 1892 to 1954. Return to Manhattan for a leisurely dinner at one of the many fine restaurants.

Day 3

Take an early morning walk up Broadway to Fifth Avenue. View New York's most famous skyscraper, the Empire State Building. Travel to the 86th floor and take a bird's-eye view of Manhattan on the outdoor observation deck. Hail a taxi cab and travel to West 45th Street. Experience a matinee at New York's oldest Baroque-style theater, Lyceum Theater. Next, enjoy "the heart of New York," Rockefeller Center. This complex integrates offices, shops, entertainment, dining, and gardens. There is always plenty to do here.

Day 4

Sightsee by city bus as you travel to the South Street Seaport and Civic Center. View historic ships docked alongside the pier. Then, get ready for a historic walk across the Brooklyn Bridge, the largest suspension bridge and the first to be constructed of steel. Return to the Seaport area and visit Schermerhorns Row—-lots of shops and restaurants.

Day 5

Take a short walk to Jones Street and have breakfast at Caffe Vivaldi, a favorite spot for delicious sticky pastries. Travel via city bus to 42nd Street, and take in the sights of the world-famous Times Square. Walk east on 42nd Street and enter the New York Public Library. Be sure to take your time in here to view the beautifully carved white marble throughout this award-winning building. Next, travel on the 1, 2, 3, or 9 subway train to Lincoln Center. Receive a backstage tour of both Lincoln Center and Carnegie Hall. Conclude the day on Pier 86 and visit the Intrepid Sea-Air Space Museum. This World War II U.S. aircraft carrier, control room, and flight deck are open for exploration.

Day 6

You are tired and exhausted. The morning is reserved for last minute souvenir shopping or a leisurely stroll down the many New York avenues. Be checked out of the hotel by 10:30 A.M. and board the Carey Airport Express bus by 10:45 A.M. Board Up and Away Airlines Flight #235 at 12:30 P.M. Arrive at Los Angeles International Airport at 5:35 P.M.

Grades 4-6

Shared Reading 47
Taking a Bite Out of the BIG APPLE

Areas of Study
Language Arts, Social Studies

Title of Shared Reading
Taking a Bite Out of the BIG APPLE
By Karen Bunnell

Text Structure
Travel Itinerary

Primary Purpose
To help the students learn to read and interpret itineraries

To teach, review, and reinforce information on historical points of interest and curricular units of study

Lessons
First Reading Focus:
To Develop Understanding

- This particular shared reading should be read in parts over several days.

- Before showing the students the text, read the title. Ask the students to make predictions about the text, based on their background knowledge.

- Explain to the class that they will be taking an imaginary journey to New York City, New York. Ask them if anyone in the class has visited New York City. Allow the students to share their travel experiences.

- Talk about the term "Big Apple" as being a nickname for New York City.

- Display the text. Ask the students what they notice about how the text is arranged on the page. Explain that one portion is a travel ticket, while the rest of the text provides an itinerary for the imaginary journey.

- Together read the ticket. Clarify specialized vocabulary, such as *transferable, itinerary, confirmation, flight,* and *depart*.

- Explain the purpose of an itinerary and how to read it.

- Each new school day, read the next day's travel plan as well as the previous day's. Each day discuss, clarify, and explain unfamiliar words and information.

Additional Readings:
To Develop Strategies and Skills

Strategies

- Reread the text that is located on the ticket, starting at the top and moving left to right. Explain to the students that it is important to read the text in order, so they are able to understand the information presented.

- Reread portions of text. Ask the students to identify words or phrases that are unfamiliar to them. Discuss their meaning.

- Reread each line of text located on the ticket. Have the students restate the meaning of each line in their own words.

Skills

- Reread the text and locate words that are capitalized. Review capitalization rules by asking the students to give the reason for the word or phrase being capitalized.

- Reread the text and locate adjectives in the selection. Discuss their purpose. Read a selected portion of the text both with and without the adjectives.

Future Readings:
Other Possible Teaching Points

- Assign groups of students to research particular landmarks visited on the itinerary. Instruct them to create a large teaching poster that includes much of the historical information and details of the landmark

Classroom Extension

- Duplicate the itinerary for each student in the class. Instruct the students to write their names next to "Passenger," and to fill in the dates for their journey. In small groups, have the students create a three-to-four day travel itinerary for the town in which they live.

Additional Resources
Berman, E. *Eyewitness Travel Guides: NEW YORK.* DK Publishing, Inc., 1999. ISBN 1564581845

Hest, A. *When Jessie Came Across the Sea.* Candlewick Press, 1997. ISBN 0763600946

Maestro, B. *The Story of the Statue of Liberty.* William Morrow & Co., 1989. ISBN 0688087469

Christopher Columbus
1145 Sailing Way
Genoa, Italy

March 13, 1492

King Ferdinand of Aragon and Queen Isabella of Castile
1 Royal Palisades
Madrid, Spain

Dear King Ferdinand and Queen Isabella:

It is well-known that Asian trade centers are among the wealthiest in the world. It has been the goal of many to establish an efficient, direct route to Asia; however, the endeavors to this point have proven futile. I believe I have a solution.

After much thorough study, I am convinced that not only is the earth round, but the most direct trade route to Asia would be to head west, across the Atlantic Ocean. The cost of such an expedition would be minimal when compared with the wealth such a direct trade route would bring. Not only riches, but consider the possibilities of acquiring new lands for the Spanish crown. Possibly the greatest benefit would be the opportunities to share our knowledge of the one, true God. It is a travesty to have such revelation and not do everything in our power to enlighten the less fortunate.

I have years of sailing experience and know how to lead; an essential skill when considering a journey of this nature in uncharted waters. My experience includes sailing on a variety of seas and oceans. I have faced and overcome every challenge encountered throughout my life on the seas. I am confident I have the skills and wisdom that only experience brings, to successfully complete this mission.

I respectfully request your aid in making such a journey possible for all of the reasons listed. As other nations are actively pursuing expeditions of similar purpose, I urge you to make all haste when deciding my fate. I will eagerly await your majesties' reply.

Your most humble servant,

Christopher Columbus

Shared Reading 48
Christopher Columbus's Letter

Areas of Study
Language Arts, Social Studies

Title of Shared Reading
Christopher Columbus's Letter
By Charlene Huntley

Text Structure
Persuasive Letter

Primary Purpose
To help the students understand the nature and purpose of persuasive documents

To identify and understand when to use a formal business letter

To understand political issues surrounding Christopher Columbus's voyage

Lessons
First Reading Focus:
To Develop Understanding
- Help the students use their background knowledge to discuss exploration. Ask them:

    Does exploration always lead to change?

    Does exploration always involve desire for wealth?

    Is exploration desirable? Are risks desirable?

- Read the letter. Discuss it and clarify any questions.

- Working in pairs, have the students ask each other questions that can be answered using the shared reading text.

- With a partner, have them summarize the first paragraph in one sentence.

- Continue reading, discussing, and summarizing each of the remaining paragraphs.

Additional Readings:
To Develop Strategies and Skills
Strategies
- Reread the text and instruct the students about persuasive business letter structure and conventions. Ask them:
    What is persuasion?
    Why would you write something persuasive?
    Can you be honest and persuasive?
    Is Columbus's argument reasonable? How did you decide?
    How does your writing change if you are trying to persuade someone?

Skills
- Reread the text and compare this persuasive business letter to other formal business letters. Expand the comparisons to friendly letters, invitations, notes, and other forms of communication. Interactively write a list of purposes and reasons for using each.

- Interactively write a persuasive letter to a school or city administrator concerning something the class feels strongly about. Display the letter for future reference.

Future Readings:
Other Possible Teaching Points
- Write a letter of support or opposition concerning Columbus's voyage, using appropriate conventions, to the king and queen of Spain.

Classroom Extension
- Research the issues surrounding Columbus's voyage. In pairs or small groups, formulate an argument for or against support of the voyage. Present the argument to the class and attempt to orally persuade them.

Additional Resources
D'Agulaire, I. *COLUMBUS*. Beautiful Feet Books, 1996. ISBN 0964380331

Dyson, J. *Westward with Columbus: Set Sail on the Voyage That Changed the World*. Scholastic, Inc., 1991. ISBN 0590438468

Spencer, E. *Three Ships for Columbus*. Raintree Steck-Vaughn Publishers, 1992. ISBN 0811472124

Columbus Sets Sail for the Ends of the Earth

Christopher Columbus has just received news that his request for aid in order to sail west to the Asian trade centers has been granted by the Spanish monarchy. The following is an interview conducted by Philip Montego of the *Spanish Inquiery Press* immediately after Columbus received the news.

PM: What prompted the idea for this voyage?

CC: It had been my dream for many years to find a route to Asia that would avoid the conflicts encountered when traveling by land. Obviously there are many advantages to finding a direct route to these wealthy trade centers. Where others have been unable to solve this problem, I believe I have the answer.

PM: Is this your first request for aid?

CC: I have requested help from other powers in Europe, but they have not grasped the vision of the benefits, such as wealth and power, a successful mission like this would bring to their countries. They have been fearful of taking risks.

PM: How long have you been trying to gain support for this mission?

CC: Too long! I have been soliciting financial support for about eight years.

PM: Why do you think you will be successful?

CC: I have meticulously studied the works of Ptolemy and others. The obvious conclusion is, not only is the earth round, but it is possible to reach the Indies by sailing straight west across the Atlantic.

PM: If you could summarize in one sentence why this endeavor is important, what would it be?

CC: I can actually sum it up in three words: wealth, expansion, and evangelism.

PM: You are Portuguese, why should Spain support you?

CC: Regardless of my nationality, the benefits for anyone supporting this mission speak for themselves.

PM: Bartholomew las Casas of the Royal Committee says, "His (Columbus's) promises and offers were impossible and vain and worthy of rejection…" How would you respond?

CC: There are always those who would like to take the conservative route and keep things as they are. If we don't take risks, how will we improve? As I said earlier, I am as certain as I can be, based upon the writings I have studied. I believe the outcome of this mission will, without doubt, establish my theories as truth.

PM: Thank you for taking time to speak with me. I know your schedule is full with preparations and plans for this voyage. We all wish you Godspeed.

Shared Reading 49
Columbus Sets Sail for the Ends of the Earth

Areas of Study
Language Arts, Social Studies

Title of Shared Reading:
Columbus Sets Sail for the Ends of the Earth
By Charlene Huntley

Text Structure
Interview

Primary Purpose
To help the students understand the nature and purpose of interviews

To help them understand issues surrounding Columbus's voyage from multiple perspectives

Lessons
First Reading Focus:
To Develop Understanding

- Help the students use their background knowledge to discuss the Age of Exploration.

- Read the interview together. Discuss and clarify any questions.

- Working with a partner, have the students ask each other questions that can be answered using the text. Write a summary statement.

- Review their summary statements and together interactively edit this interview into one sentence.

Additional Readings:
To Develop Strategies and Skills

Strategies
- Reread the text and discuss the purpose of an interview. Identify the audience. Discuss the kinds of questions to include in an interview.

- Reread the text, concentrating on the layout. How and why do the formats and conventions change for recording an interview in writing?

Skills
- Reread the text and think about what makes a good interview question. Interactively write characteristics of a good interview question.

- Interactively write sample interview questions.

Future Readings:
Other Possible Teaching Points

- Listen to or view a short, taped interview. Note and discuss the characteristics of the questions and the interview topic. As a class, record the interview in writing, using appropriate conventions.

Classroom Extension

- Have the students choose a controversial topic and prepare interview questions. Then have them critique the questions with a partner. Have them interview a person and record the interview in writing, using appropriate conventions, for a magazine.

Additional Resources
Columbus, C. *The Log of Christopher Columbus's First Voyage to America: In The Year 1492 as Copied by His Companion.* Shoe String Press, 1997. ISBN 0208022473

Conrad, P. *Pedro's Journal: A Voyage with Christopher Columbus.* Scholastic, 1992. ISBN 0590462067

Yolen, J. *Encounter.* Harcourt, 1996. ISBN 015201389X

The Star Spangled Banner

Oh, say, can you see, by the dawn's early light,

What so proudly we hail'd at the twilight's last gleaming?

Whose broad stripes and bright stars, thro' the perilous fight,

O'er the ramparts we watch'd, were so gallantly streaming?

And the rockets' red glare, the bombs bursting in air,

Gave proof thro' the night that our flag was still there.

O say, does that star-spangled banner yet wave

O'er the land of the free and the home of the brave?

Shared Reading 50
The Star Spangled Banner

Areas of Study
Language Arts, Social Studies

Title of Shared Reading
The Star Spangled Banner
By Francis Scott Key

Text Structure
Song

Primary Purpose
To allow students to discuss their understanding of a familiar song

To encourage patriotism by developing a deeper understanding of a familiar song

A student-illustrated class book.

Lessons
First Reading Focus:
To Develop Understanding

- Have the students become familiar with the selection by singing the text many times without the printed copy available.

- Introduce the text by having the students read the title and asking them to share what they know about the song "The Star Spangled Banner."

- Sing the text, inviting the students to sing along with you. Then read the text, again inviting them to participate by reading with you. Point to the edge of each line of text while reading to help the students track the print.

Additional Readings:
To Develop Strategies and Skills

Strategies
- Reread the text. Ask the students to think about the author of the text and the message he was trying to convey, and his feelings about his flag and his country. Encourage the students to return to the text to provide evidence to support their ideas.

- Reread the text, phrase by phrase. Ask the students to restate the meaning of each phrase in their own words.

Skills
- Locate various vocabulary that the students may not understand. Using the context of the text, as well as background knowledge about the origin and background of the text, try to determine word meanings. Use a dictionary to check the students' predictions.

- On different days, locate examples of adjectives, adverbs, and verbs in the text. Discuss how these words add to the text and enable the reader to create more vibrant mental images as they read. Encourage the students to use these types of words in their own writing.

Future Readings:
Other Possible Teaching Points
- Locate words that contain apostrophes. Discuss the reasons for the use of the apostrophes in each word.

- Compare this song to other patriotic songs, such as "America the Beautiful." Ask the students to summarize the ideas or feelings expressed, and contrast them to those expressed in "The Star Spangled Banner."

Classroom Extensions
- Use interactive writing to create a Venn diagram that compares and contrasts two patriotic songs. The students may use this resource when writing an independent piece that compares and contrasts the two songs.

- Use interactive editing to change the text of "The Star Spangled Banner" to a narrative or expository text.

Additional Resources
Ayer, E. *Our Flag.* Millbrook Press, 1994. ISBN 1878841866

Kroll, S. *By the Dawn's Early Light (The Story of The Star Spangled Banner).* Scholastic, 1994. ISBN 0590450557

Williams, R. *What You Should Know About the American Flag.* Thomas Publications, 1989. ISBN 0939631105

True Friends

Narrator: A boy was cleaning out his bedroom, and his eyes popped out of his head when he found a five-dollar bill under this bed.

Buck: WOW! Just think, I was down in the dumps because I had to do my chores!

Narrator: This good fortune helped the boy finish his chores ahead of time. He quickly ran downstairs to tell his mom.

Buck: Surprise! No more song and dance needed to get me to clean my room. It's spic-n-span.

Mom: It seems like you are walking on air, now that your room is FINALLY clean. Huh?

Buck: Yah! Can I go hang out at Penny's?

Mom: Well, now that your room is taken care of, I suppose you have rollerblading on the brain. Go ahead, but be home for dinner by six o'clock.

Narrator: Buck's head was in the clouds as he rapidly skated over to his best friend's house. He knocked on Penny's front door.

Penny: Hi, Buck! I thought cleaning your room would take you forever and a day!

Buck: Me too! But this five-dollar bill came out of nowhere when I was cleaning, and it inspired me to get down to business.

Penny: So, you've had that five dollars for what—fifteen minutes—and it's burning a hole in your pocket already?

Buck: No... Well, yeah!! You helped me study for the math test, so I owe you one. Let's go all out and go over to the candy shop and take advantage of my good fortune. C'mon!

Penny: Candy?... Spend it?... Alright! You drive a hard bargain!

Narrator: Buck and Penny's rollerblades hugged the road as they blazed over to the local mall.

Buck: I have to be home by six o'clock, so let's stick together so we don't waste time.

Penny: O.K. Hey! Hold your horses! Take a look at that book in the store window.

Buck: You have a fat chance of getting me to spend this money on a BOOK!!

Penny: Never mind. They are asking an arm and a leg for it, anyways.

Narrator: Penny walks into the bookstore and motions for Buck to follow her.

Penny: Buck, maybe it's time to turn over a new leaf and decide what kind of book you enjoy reading.

Buck: BOOKS are for the birds!!

Penny: Do you have any more half-baked ideas? Everyone should enjoy reading. You're not out of the woods yet, Buck. Let's take a look over there on the bargain table.

Buck: O.K. I get the picture!! You won't leave here until I at least look at these books, right?

Narrator: Penny nods her head, and they begin fishing for books at the bargain table.

Buck: Keep it under your hat, Penny, but I did enjoy that movie *Indian in the Cupboard*, and I would like to read that book.

Penny: I'll go and see if one of the store clerks can lay his hands on that book. Be right back.

Narrator: Within minutes, Penny turns up with the book *Indian in the Cupboard* and hands it over to Buck.

Buck: Gee, thanks.

Penny: It's only three dollars and ninety-five cents. Plus the tax, of course. So cough up the money or eat your words, Buck. HA! HA!

Buck: Well, I guess the ball is in my court now.

Narrator: Buck and Penny don't always see eye to eye. However, this story goes to show you, true friends take to heart the words spoken to one another.

Shared Reading 51
True Friends

Area of Study
Language Arts

Title of Shared Reading
True Friends
By Karen Bunnell

Text Structure
Reader's Theater Script

Primary Purpose
To practice reading and interpreting a script

To understand idiomatic expressions through the context of a literary work

Lessons
First Reading Focus:
To Develop Understanding
- Reproduce enough scripts so that each student has a copy. Explain to the class that this is the text of a short play.

- Discuss the format and structure of the text.

- Read the entire script together, including the names of the characters for the first reading. Pause after every few lines to clarify and discuss what is happening in the play.

- Reread the script as dialogue without reading the characters' names.

- Prompt the students to look carefully at the language used in the script.

- Define, or help the students define, an idiom. Entertain questions and ideas about the many idiomatic expressions in the script.

Additional Readings:
To Develop Strategies and Skills
Strategies
- Reread the entire script together for several days, focusing on fluency, phrasing, and expression.

- Divide the class into four groups: Narrator, Mom, Buck, and Penny. Have each student highlight his or her dialogue.

- Allow the four groups time to individually practice their dialogue.

- Come together as a group and read the script.

- Repeat the same procedure, but rotate the groups and roles.

Skills
- Reread the script, and locate and highlight all idiomatic words or phrases. Discuss the literal meanings versus the author's intent in using these expressions.

Future Readings:
Other Possible Teaching Points
- Rewrite the script, replacing the idioms with literal translations.

Classroom Extension
- Perform the play for other classes.

Additional Resources
Juster, N. *The Phantom Tollbooth*. Alfred A. Knopf Publishers, 1971. ISBN 0394820371

Lowry, L. *The Giver*. Houghton Mifflin, 1993. ISBN 0395645662

Sachar, L. *Holes*. Bantam Doubleday Dell Books for Young Readers, 2000. ISBN 0440414806

Terban, M. *Mad as a Wet Hen: And other Funny Idioms*. Houghton Mifflin, 1987. ISBN 0899194796

Terban, M. *The Scholastic Dictionary of Idioms*. Scholastic, Inc., 1998. ISBN 0590381571

The Bremen Town Musicians

CAST

Group 1: Narrator 1

Group 2: Narrator 2

Group 3: Man

Group 4: Francis, the talking mule

Group 5: Rooster

Group 6: Dandy Dog

Group 7: Morris, the cat

Group 8: Robber A

Group 9: Robber B

SET-UP

The children have their own copies of the script and stand in various locations around the room. Groups are typically 4-5 children.

Narrator 1: This is the story of "The Bremen Town Musicians." It is a story about some animals that decided to become musicians.

Narrator 2: Once upon a time, there lived an old man and his talking mule, named Francis.

Man: Francis, I don't know what to do with you. You can't pull a plow, and you're too old to carry anything heavy.

Mule: Hee-ho, hee-haw. Hee-ho, hee-haw. I'm so tired. Maybe some vitamins would help.

Narrator 2: The old man was very sad.

Man: I can't afford to feed you anymore. Guess I'll have to sell you to Elmer's® glue factory.

Mule: (Scared) Hee-haw, hee-haw. Oh, what will I do? I'm not eligible for my pension yet.

Narrator 2: That night, the mule decided to run away. So he packed his gym bag.

Mule: Clippity, clop, clippity clop, clippity, clippity, clop.

Narrator 1: He left for Bremen, in the L.A. Valley.

Narrator 2: Early the next morning …

Rooster: Cock-a-doodle-doo. Cock-a-doodle-doo.

Narrator 2: The old man went to his barn to get his mule.

Man: Now, where did Francis vanish to (emphasize the word *vanish*)?

Narrator 1: The old man was flushed from ear to ear.

Man: I wish he hadn't vanished. I decided to keep him after all.

Narrator 1: What a revolting predicament this is!

Narrator 2: That same morning, the mule hadn't gone far, when he saw a dog.

Mule: Hello. What are you eating?

Dog: Chicken and cheese, chicken and cheese. All I want is my doggie chicken and cheese.

Mule: Why are you by the roadside?

Dog: My name might be Dandy, but I'm no longer handy. My master doesn't want me, so I ran away.

Mule: I'm going to Bremen to become a town musician. Come along with me and be one, too.

Narrator 2: The dog thought this was a good idea, so they both went down to the freeway.

Dog & Mule: Clippity clop, clippity clop, clippity, clippity, clop.

Narrator 1: A short time later,

Narrator 2: they came upon a cat.

Cat: (Sings) Meow, meow, meow, meow, meow, meow, meow, meow, meow, meow, meow, meow, meow, meow, meow, meow.

Mule: Hello. What is your name?

Cat: Morris.

Dog: He looks familiar.

Cat: My owner thinks I'm too old to chase mice, so she threw me out of her motor home.

Mule: We're going to Bremen to become town musicians.

Dog: (Sings) Come along with me, I'm on my way to the stars.

Narrator 1:	So the three animals continued the journey to worlds unknown.
Mule, Dog, and Cat:	Clippity clop, clippity clop, clippity, clippity, clop.
Narrator 2:	That evening, as they came to Redlands, they heard a terrible noise.
Rooster:	(Loudly) Cock-a-doodle-doo!
Cat:	What was that?
Dog:	I think it's Rooster sitting on that gate.
Rooster:	Cock-a-doodle-doop. My master wants me in his bowl of soup.
Mule:	Rooster, why are you so unhappy?
Rooster:	My master needs some chicken for his noodle soup, and I'm it!
Mule:	We're going to Bremen to become town musicians.
Cat:	You have a strong voice.
Dog:	Come along with us.
Narrator 2:	So all four animals went off together.
Animals:	Clippity clop, clippity clop, clippity, clippity, clop.
Narrator 1:	Later that night …
Mule:	[Glancing at his watch] Rooster, my watch says it's time for my favorite TV show.
Dog:	We need to rest.
Cat:	Can you find us a nice place?
Narrator 2:	So Rooster flew a big plane around and around, until he saw a nearby light.
Narrator 1:	Soon they came to a two-story house.
Dog:	It's not a hotel.
Cat:	But it will do for tonight.
Rooster:	I wonder who lives here.
Mule:	I'll climb near the windows and peek.
Dog and Cat:	(Sing) Are you hungry, are you hungry, for a hamburger right now?

Rooster:	I wish I had some pepperoni pizza.
Narrator 1:	So they thought up a plan.
Narrator 2:	The dog climbed up on the mules back,
Narrator 1:	and the cat climbed up on the dog's back,
Narrator 2:	and Rooster stood on the cat's head.
Narrator 1:	All at once …
All Four Animals:	Hee, haw, bow-wow, meow, cock-a-doodle-doo, hee, haw, bow-wow, meow, cock-a-doodle-doo.
Narrator 2:	The robbers were afraid the Highway Patrol had caught them.
Robber A:	Leapin' lizards!
Robber B:	Run for your life!
Robber A:	Let me out of here!
Narrator 2:	Afterward, the animals went into the house and had a feast.
Narrator 1:	Soon, they all went to sleep.
Mule:	Good night, Dandy dog.
Dog:	Good night, Morris.
Cat:	Good night, Rooster.
Rooster:	Good night, Francis.
Narrator 2:	The moral of this story isn't certain, 'cause it's not over yet! Later that night, the robbers returned.
Robber A:	The front light isn't on anymore.
Robber B:	Let's sneak back into the house.
Narrator 1:	Just then, they woke a startled Rooster.
Rooster: (Very loudly)	Cock-a-doodle-doo! Cock-a-doodle-doo!
Narrator 2:	In the darkness, one robber stepped on the cat's tail.
Cat:	Meow! (Scratch) Meow! (Scratch)
Narrator 1:	The other robber ran for the door, kicked the dog, and was bitten on the leg.

(continued)

The Bremen Town Musicians (continued)

Dog: Grrrr, growl,
Grrrr, growl.

Narrator 2: As the robbers ran across the yard, the mule kicked them both as hard as he could.

Everyone: Crunch!

Narrator 1: The next day in Bremen, everyone listened to two men telling a strange tale about a terrible monster.

Robber A: She scratched me with her long fingernails.

Robber B: And shrieked louder than the thunder.

Robber A: With teeth sharper than razors.

Robber B: And so strong, she threw us across the yard.

Narrator 2: And the...

Mule: Hee-haw.

Narrator 2: And the...

Dog: Grrrr, grrrr.

Narrator 2: And the...

Cat: Meow, meow.

Narrator 2: And the...

Rooster: Cock-a-doodle-doo.

Narrator 2: The animals lived happily ever after.

Narrator 1: The moral to this story so old
Can now be told.
Without teamwork,
No one could be bold.

Shared Reading 52
The Bremen Town Musicians

Area of Study
Language Arts

Title of Shared Reading
The Bremen Town Musicians
Retold by Adria F. Klein

Text Structure
Reader's Theater Script

Primary Purpose
To practice reading and interpreting a script

To provide opportunities for oral presentation

Lessons
First Reading Focus:
To Develop Understanding

- Reproduce the text on an overhead transparency. As you display the first page, explain that this is the text of a short play. Discuss the fact that some portions of the text will be read aloud, while other parts will be read and interpreted silently.

- Ask the students to listen and watch as you read the text aloud. Point to the names of the characters as you read the dialogue of the text. Use different voices for each character.

- After the reading, clarify with the students which portions of the text are read aloud and which are read silently. Return to the portions of the text that were read silently. Read the different sections aloud, and explain the different purposes for each. Clarify any unfamiliar vocabulary or concepts.

- Reread the text, inviting the students to join you. Encourage them to read with expression.

Additional Readings:
To Develop Strategies and Skills

Strategies
- Reproduce enough scripts so that each student has a copy. Highlight the portions of text that are read aloud. Reread the entire script together for several days, focusing on fluency and expression. Point out the sections in parentheses, which give directions for appropriate expression.

- Divide the class into nine groups: Narrator 1, Narrator 2, Man, Francis the talking mule, Rooster, Dandy Dog, Morris the cat, Robber A and Robber B.

- Give the groups time to work together to practice their dialogue.

- Come together as a group to read the script. Begin by simply reading the dialogue.

Skills
- Reread the script. Locate the text that is set aside as stage directions. Highlight this text in a different color. Discuss the use of parentheses.

- Look for examples of onomatopoeia in the text. Discuss how these words add to the text.

- Locate examples of proper nouns and common nouns in the text. Discuss the difference between common and proper nouns, as well as the need to capitalize proper nouns.

- Discuss the repetitive nature of the text. Ask the students to think of other stories they know that work the same way.

Future Readings:
Other Possible Teaching Points

- Use interactive editing to rewrite the script as a narrative.

- Find examples of proper nouns in the text. Using an interactive editing technique, ask the students to change those to proper nouns that are more meaningful to them.

- Read aloud another version of *The Bremen Town Musicians*. Compare and contrast the different versions.

Classroom Extensions
- Perform the play for parents, an assembly, or other classrooms.

- Allow the students to create masks, hats, or props to use during their performance.

Additional Resources
Bauer, C. *Presenting Reader's Theatre: Plays and Poems to Read Aloud*. H.W. Wilson Company, 1987. ISBN 0824207483

Trussell-Cullen, A. *The Musicians of Bremen (The Dominie Collection of Traditional Tales, Set 2)*. Dominie Press, 2002. ISBN 0768503329

Shared Reading Is for Everyone

The principal shares a favorite book.

The teacher uses an overhead projector.

A visitor gets in on the act.

Children love shared reading.

7. Literacy Skills Checklist

The Literacy Skills Checklist is provided as a resource for teachers to record skill acquisition for each child. This checklist is not designed to be used as a test.

The source of this information is the teacher's observation of reading and writing behaviors in classroom activities. There is no regular order in which children will exhibit these skills.

When using with older students, use only the skill level that applies to the students at their grade level.

NOTE: this checklist may be duplicated for each child.

Alphabet
NOTE: Assess the children's ability to recognize, locate, name and form letters prior to instruction so that you can tailor your teaching to each child's needs.

Recognizes, locates, and names letters (Circle those the child knows.)

a b c d e f g h i j k l m n o p q r s t u v w x y z
A B C D E F G H I J K L M N O P Q R S T U V W X Y Z

Forms letters (Circle those the child has mastered.)

a b c d e f g h i j k l m n o p q r s t u v w x y z
A B C D E F G H I J K L M N O P Q R S T U V W X Y Z

Sings or recites the alphabet (with or without a model)

Phonemic Awareness (✔ check when demonstrated)
- ☐ Claps syllables in words
- ☐ Counts syllables in multisyllabic words
- ☐ Recognizes rhymes
- ☐ Produces rhyme
- ☐ Blends segmented sounds to say words
- ☐ Blends different beginning sounds with phonograms (onset and rime)
- ☐ Segments sounds in monosyllabic words
- ☐ Manipulates sounds by substituting one sound for another
- ☐ Manipulates sounds by adding or subtracting one sound for another

Phonics
Associates alphabet letters with these basic sounds (Circle those the child has mastered.)

b /b/	c /k/	d /d/	f /f/	g /g/	h /h/
j /j/	k /k/	l /l/	m /m/	n /n/	p /p/
q /kw/	r /r/	s /s/	t /t/	v /v/	w /w/
x /ks/	y /y/	z /z/			

Recognizes short vowel sounds (Circle those the child knows.)

a   e   i   o   u

Recognizes long vowel sounds (Circle those the child knows.)

/a/   /e/   /i/   /o/   /u/

Reads and locates words with these vowel letter-sound correspondences
(Circle those the child regularly decodes in words.)

ai /a/	ay /a/	ea /e/	ee /e/	oa /o/
ow	oo	oo /oo/	oi /oi/	oy /oi/
ou /ou/	ow /ou/	ar	er /ir/ /ur/	or

Recognizes alternative sounds of consonant letters. (Circle those the child knows.)

| c /s/ | g /j/ | wh /hw/ |
| ch /ch/ | sh /sh/ | th /th/ |

Reads and locates words with these initial consonant blends. (Circle those the child knows.)

br	cr	dr	fr	gr	pr	tr	wr
bl	cl	fl	gl	pl	sl		
sc	sk	sm	sn	sp	st	sw	
scr	squ	str	spr	spl	shr	sch	
dw	tw	thr					

Reads and locates words with these final consonant blends (Circle those the child knows.)

| ct | ft | lt | nt | pt | rt | st |
| ld | nd | rd | nk | sk | mp | nc(e) |

Print Awareness
(✔ check when demonstrated)

☐ Locates the front of a book

☐ Recognizes that print is what is read on a page

☐ Can point out where text begins (top left)

☐ Follows a line of print from left to right

☐ Moves from right-hand end of one line to left-hand beginning of next

☐ Points to each word as it is read

☐ Recognizes when sentences begin and end

☐ Understands that a question mark indicates a sentence asks a question

☐ Understands that an exclamation mark indicates the sentence should be read with excitement or surprise

☐ Understands the quotation marks come before and after words said by a character

Reading Skills

Reads and locates high-frequency words (Circle those the child recognizes with regularity.)

a	about	all	an	and	are
as	at	be	been	but	by
call	can	come	could	day	did
do	down	each	find	first	for
from	get	go	had	has	have
he	her	him	his	how	I
if	in	into	is	it	its
like	long	look	made	make	many
may	more	my	no	not	now
number	of	oil	on	one	or
other	out	part	people	said	see
she	so	some	than	that	the
their	them	then	there	these	they
this	time	to	two	up	use
was	water	way	we	were	what
when	which	who	will	with	word
would	write	you	your		

(✔ check when demonstrated)

☐ Reads and locates words with short a, as in cap

☐ Reads and locates words with short e, as in bed

☐ Reads and locates words with short i, as in trip

☐ Reads and locates words with short o, as in box

☐ Reads and locates words with short u, as in rug

☐ Reads and locates words with long a
- ☐ spelled a as in paper
- ☐ spelled a-consonant-e as in game
- ☐ spelled ai as in rain
- ☐ spelled ay as in play

☐ Reads and locates words with long e
- ☐ spelled e as in eat
- ☐ spelled ee as in feed
- ☐ spelled e-consonant-e as in delete
- ☐ spelled e as in he
- ☐ spelled eo as in people

☐ Reads and locates words with long i
- ☐ spelled i as in like
- ☐ spelled ie as in tried
- ☐ spelled y as in my
- ☐ spelled i as in Ice

☐ Reads and locates words with long o
- ☐ spelled o-consonant-o as in home
- ☐ spelled oa as in road
- ☐ spelled ow as in mow
- ☐ spelled oe as in toe
- ☐ spelled o as in go
- ☐ spelled oh

☐ Reads and locates words with long u
- ☐ spelled u-consonant-u as in tune
- ☐ spelled ue as in Tuesday
- ☐ spelled u as in music
- ☐ spelled eau as in beautiful
- ☐ spelled oo as in noon
- ☐ spelled ou as in youth
- ☐ spelled o as in who

Strategies for Reading
(✔ check when demonstrated)

- ☐ Directionality
- ☐ One-to-one matching
- ☐ Return sweep
- ☐ Concept of first and last part of word, sentence, story
- ☐ Locating known and unknown words
- ☐ Searching for sources of information to problem solve at point of difficulty
- ☐ Self-correction

Written Language and Concept Development
(✔ check those the child recognizes, locates and reads)

- ☐ Punctuation
- ☐ Spelling and word analysis
- ☐ Sentence structure
- ☐ Grammar
- ☐ Parts of speech
- ☐ Irregular words
- ☐ Contractions
- ☐ Antonyms
- ☐ Synonyms
- ☐ Homographs
- ☐ Homophones
- ☐ Metaphors
- ☐ Similes
- ☐ Idioms

Comprehension
Structural features of informational materials
(✔ check those the child is able to recognize, locate and read)

- ☐ Title
- ☐ Table of contents
- ☐ Author
- ☐ Illustrator
- ☐ Chapter headings
- ☐ Glossary
- ☐ Index

(✔ check those the child is able to read and interpret)

- ☐ Information from diagrams, charts, captions and graphs
- ☐ Sequence, chronological order
- ☐ Cause and effect
- ☐ Fact and opinion

Structural features of literary materials

(✔ check those the child is able to read and interpret)

☐ Styles of literature (including poetry, drama, fiction, and nonfiction, fantasies, fables, myths, legends, fairy tales)

☐ Strategies of reading for different purposes

☐ Sequence

☐ Figurative language

☐ Sentence structure

☐ Rhythm

Comprehension and analysis

(✔ check those the child is able to recognize, locate and use)

☐ Pictures, context, captions, charts, maps, and graphs to determine unknown words and make predictions

☐ Confirm or discount predictions in order to make new predictions or modify predictions

☐ Who, what, when, where, why, and how questions

☐ Written directions (e.g. one step, two step, multiple steps)

☐ Key words

☐ Clarifying questions

☐ Restate facts and details

☐ Connect to life experiences

☐ Relate prior knowledge to text

☐ Retell familiar stories, expository, narrative passages

☐ Inferences

☐ Main idea and supporting details

Narrative Analysis

(✔ check those the child is able to recognize and read)

☐ Fantasy versus reality

☐ Types of everyday print

☐ Plot, character, setting and important events

☐ Theme or moral in a selected text

☐ Author's purpose

☐ Identify the speaker and recognize the difference between first and third person narration

8. Shared Reading Procedural Checklist and Self-assessment

Before The Reading

Are the students already familiar with the shared reading, or is it a new piece?

_____

Why was the shared reading selection chosen?   ✔ Check all that apply.

☐ Teacher Choice: to directly and explicitly teach a strategy or skill.

☐ Strategic Choice: to teach, demonstrate, or clarify a point of confusion.

☐ Content Area Theme: to support the current unit of study.

☐ Specialized Uses: to give direction (management, rules, etc.) or transition from oral language to print (songs, chants, etc.).

Planning for the Lesson

What observations and/or assessment guided your choice of the shared reading?

_____

_____

What trends are you noticing in one student or a group of students that may need more clarifying and further teaching to help resolve confusions?

_____

_____

What is your primary objective for this lesson?

_____

_____

Which standards, skills, strategies, and comprehension issues can be addressed as you revisit this shared reading on other occasions?

_____

_____

What print already in the room will support you in connecting your teaching points to previous lessons? List examples.

☐ Word Wall _____	☐ Name Chart _____
☐ Interactive Writing _____	☐ ABC Chart _____
☐ Interactive Editing Pieces _____	☐ Content Texts _____
☐ Other Shared Readings _____	☐ Informational Charts _____
☐ Literacy Centers _____	☐ Graphs _____

What text structure was the shared reading?

☐ Poem	☐ Content Area	☐ Math Problem	☐ Chart
☐ Letter	☐ Reader's Theater	☐ Directions	☐ Rules
☐ Graph	☐ Song	☐ Definitions	☐ Dialogue
☐ Story	☐ List	☐ Chant	☐ Other

During the Reading

How did you make your main teaching points both direct and explicit?

_____

_____

What confusions or uncertainties did the students have that became apparent during this lesson?

_____

_____

How were connections to previous learning made?

_____

_____

How was the text reread?

☐ Word by Word   ☐ Phrase by Phrase for Fluency   ☐ As a Complete Piece

What strategies, skills, and comprehension issues were you able to directly reinforce during this lesson?

☐ Strategies	☐ Cross-checking	☐ Phonemic Awareness and Phonics	☐ Rereading
☐ Locating Known and Unknown Words	☐ Self-correcting	☐ Written Language Conventions	☐ Questioning
☐ Monitoring	☐ Skills	☐ Comprehension	☐ Fluency
☐ Searching	☐ Alphabetic Principle		☐ Grammar
	☐ Concepts about Print		☐ Other

How was engagement sustained?

_____

_____

What classroom management techniques were used (songs, chants, redirecting, focusing)?

_____

_____

List specific prompts used to help the students transfer skills from shared reading to their own independent work. (For example: What can you do to help yourself? If you were working by yourself, what would you try? Would any of the words on the word wall help us? Read that again and see if it sounds right to you.)

_____

_____

After The Reading

Considering your teaching points, which would be the best places for the students to practice what you presented? Site specific instances.

☐ Interactive Writing _____

☐ Independent Writing _____

☐ Interactive Editing _____

☐ Literacy Centers _____

☐ Guided Reading _____

☐ Independent Reading _____

☐ Read Aloud _____

☐ Other Shared Readings _____

With what activity did you follow the lesson in order to help the students take their new learning to immediate practice?

_____

_____

Is there another shared reading piece you can choose that will also illustrate your teaching point and give your students additional reinforcement on this standards, skills, strategies, or comprehension issue?

_____

_____

Possible Teaching Points for Shared Reading

These teaching points can be addressed using shared readings from various content area texts in language arts, mathematics, science, and social studies.

Alphabetic Principle

- Letter recognition
- Letter formation
- Letter-name correspondence
- Letter-sound correspondence
- Alphabetic order

Concepts about Print

- Directionality
- One-to-one matching
- Return sweep
- Spacing, indentation, paragraph form, charts, and text layout
- Concept of first and last part of word, sentence, and story
- Punctuation, reading the punctuation

Phonemic Awareness and Phonics

- Hearing sounds in words
- Inflectional endings
- Rhyming
- Syllabication
- Compound words
- Onset and rime
- Segmentation
- Chunking and blending
- Root words
- Sounds in sequence
- Analogies
- High frequency words
- Spelling patterns
- Consonants, blends, short and long vowels, digraphs, and diphthongs
- Alliteration
- Suffixes, prefixes, and root words

Written Language Conventions

- Punctuation and capitalization
- Spelling and word analysis
- Sentence structure
- Grammar
- Proofreading and editing
- Parts of speech
- Word usage
- Irregular words
- Onomatopoeia
- Contractions
- Metaphors and similes
- Idioms

Advanced Reading Skills

- Fluency
- Text structure
- Word study
- Comprehension
- Predicting
- Understanding main idea and themes
- Summarizing
- Cause and effect
- Inferring
- Synthesizing

Appendix A
Writing Your Own Shared Readings

One of the most challenging aspects of shared reading is finding just the right text to meet specific teaching purposes. There are many resources available for obtaining shared reading text, such as literature that has been read aloud, the interactive writings that the class has created, content area books, reference materials, textbooks, magazines, poetry, and song books.

The teacher may also want to consider writing original text for shared reading. This can be an effective method for incorporating the strategies and skills that need to be addressed in the classroom. Older students may also participate in this process, giving them ownership of the piece. The following ideas are examples to provide the teacher with a variety of ways to get started.

Rewriting Text Using an Old Favorite Song or Poem

All students have favorite songs and poems that they love to sing and chant. Using these old favorites, rewritten with key words from current units of study, will provide fun ways to participate in reading and review concepts and information. First, begin with the needs of the students: What strategies and skills need additional work? Next, using standards as a guide, determine a content area of study. Integration of strategy and skill work with content area instruction provides connected and meaningful learning for students—and less work for the teacher.

Choose a favorite song or poem that is familiar to the students. Begin by identifying key words from the area of study. Review the list and look for words that fit the pattern of the original piece, substituting these words to create a shared reading text. Occasionally the teacher may choose to break from the existing pattern. The following are actual classroom examples.

I'm a Little Teapot
I'm a little teapot;
Short and stout.
Here is my handle,
Here is my spout.
When I get all steamed up,
Hear me shout.
Tip me over,
Pour me out.

I'm a Big First Grader
I'm a big first grader,
Good and smart.
Here is my brain,
The hard working part.
When I get to school,
I'm ready to start.
I'll work real hard,
With all my heart.

This poem was created for a group of beginning first graders. The teacher's purpose was to reinforce early reading behaviors: one-to-one matching, directionality, left to right and return sweep, and locating known words, while combining instruction in a thematic unit of study about self.

This is another example of rewriting an old favorite song into a new text that can be used as shared reading to reinforce early reading behaviors.

This Land is Your Land

By Woody Guthrie

This land is your land,
This land is my land,
From California,
To the New York islands
From the redwood forest,
To the Gulf Stream waters,
This land was made for you and me.

This School is Your School

This school is your school,
This school is my school.
From the cafeteria,
Out to the playground,
From my classroom,
Down to the office,
This school was made for you and me

As a culminating unit activity, older students may participate, with the teacher rewriting text using the format of an old favorite. This would serve to summarize and review unit concepts while applying written language skills to create a shared reading piece.

Fourth grade students rewrote this poem with their teacher after studying states and capitals. Comprehension skills were applied as words were strategically chosen to carry meaning. The students practiced revision and editing skills. Since they enjoyed reading the poem together, all the students practiced fluent reading on a variety of text level formats.

Pawpaw Patch

Where, oh where is sweet little Mary,
Where, oh where is sweet little Mary,
Where, oh where is sweet little Mary?
Way down yonder in the pawpaw patch.
Picking up pawpaws,
Putting them in her pocket,
Picking up pawpaws,
Putting them in her pocket,
Way down yonder in the pawpaw patch.

States and Capitals

What's the capital of (insert name of state)
What's the capital of (insert name of state)
What's the capital of (insert name of state)
Everybody take a guess.
It's the hub, of the state,
Making laws to guide our fate.
Hurry now,
It's getting late,
What's the capital of the state?

Original Poems, Prose, Songs, and Chants

The teacher might want to write a poem to use as a shared reading text by creating a frame. First consider the current unit of study and brainstorm content vocabulary words. Decide what the teacher frame will look like: Will every line rhyme, every other line rhyme, or will there be no rhyme at all? Sometimes the pattern of the text becomes obvious as the message is worked out for the shared reading. This may involve several revisions as the teacher finds something that works for the classroom.

I Love to Swing

I like to run,
I like to hop,
I love to swing,
I just can't stop.

I go up high,
I go down low,
To stop the swing,
I drag my toe.

If I hold on tight,
And really try,
When I close my eyes,
I can almost fly.

This primary grade teacher decided to write a poem using high frequency words the students were using daily. She wrote about a swing, something all students have experienced.

Another example used in a second grade classroom supports a social studies unit on ancestors. Again, the teacher identified key words: *family tree, ancestors, past, choices,* and *future*. She brainstormed words to rhyme with family tree (*bee, see, me, free, key, he, we, be, gee, three, knee*). As she put these together, she came up with phrases like "blazed the trail" and "came before me." She continued the process to create an original piece.

My Family Tree

When I look back,
At my family tree.
I get a little peek,
At what makes up me.

All my ancestors
Who came before me,
Helped blaze the trail,
For what I can be.

The choices they made,
Are part of the key,
To a bright, bright future,
For my family and me.

Older students may work together with the teacher to create an original piece, reflecting their thoughts, feelings, and understandings of the unit of study. This would be considered an interactive writing that evolves into a shared reading. The shared reading can be used for many repeated rereadings. The skills practiced in the interactive writing and the shared reading provide a link to word study and independent writing and reading.

Expository Text

Expository texts can also be used to create a shared reading. Depending on student needs and curricular requirements, shared reading becomes a tool for teaching comprehension and decoding strategies as well as exposure to a variety of text formats and structures. Students can be taught through shared reading to strategically read a variety of genres and text formats.

When choosing to write expository text for shared reading, the teacher will want to consider the students' needs, standards, and text formats. Next, identify the essential concepts and content that the students in the grade level need to learn. Select a format that best conveys this information. Text formats could include outlines, charts, multiple paragraph reports, memos, business letters, etc. Also consider special text features (for example, font size, bold print, underlined words, italics, and special conventions of print).

After participating in discussions, reading textbook selections, and listening to a variety of read alouds, an intermediate teacher wrote the following piece to demonstrate how text can be organized into a format that helps the reader summarize information.

Constitution

The Constitution creates a system of government that protects us and allows us many freedoms:

We have the right to elect our leaders.

We have the right to religious freedom.

We have the right to write or speak freely.

The laws of our country protect us from being unfairly punished or imprisoned.
All citizens of our country have the same rights.

The following intermediate example demonstrates how another teacher used a content area shared reading to introduce paragraphs and their purpose. At the same time, she was able to use this as an introduction to a unit of study on recycling. A subsequent comprehension lesson covered how to use context clues in order to understand the content vocabulary.

Recycling

Each person in the United States throws away about four pounds of garbage a day and thus is making our planet an unsafe and unhealthy place to live. We could cut down on this terrible waste by taking time to recycle.

There are many things we can learn to recycle. Many products come in glass jars. Lots of people just throw them away, but many of the bottles are returnable, so they can be reused. Some aluminum cans are also returnable, and the rest can be compressed and melted down and made into new cans. Plastic is easy to recycle because, although plastic is not biodegradable, it can be melted down and poured into new molds. People in the United States cut down millions of trees each year to make paper products. Paper is the easiest of all to recycle.

Note: When a shared reading is needed, the teacher may find that writing shared reading text is the best resource. Taking the information the teacher wants and the knowledge the students have, and combining them with skills and strategies, the teacher can create an original shared reading that is a perfect fit for the classroom. In the process, the teacher has an opportunity to model reading and writing for a number of purposes.

Appendix B

Phonics Skills Charts

Words with *ai* Phonograms

ain	air	aid	ail	ait
gain	fair	laid	bail	bait
lain	hair	maid	fail	gait
main	lair	paid	Gail	wait
pain	pair	raid	hail	trait
rain	chair	braid	jail	strait
vain	flair	staid	mail	
brain	stair	afraid	nail	
chain			pail	
grain			quail	
plain			rail	
Spain			sail	
stain			tail	
train			wail	
sprain			frail	
train			snail	
			trail	

Words with *ay* Phonograms

bay	ray	pray
day	say	spay
gay	way	stay
hay	bray	sway
jay	clay	tray
lay	flay	spray
may	fray	stray
nay	gray	away
pay	play	today

Words with *ea* Phonograms

ead	east	eat	ear	eal	ea	eak	eam
bead	beast	beat	dear	deal	lea	beak	beam
lead	feast	feat	fear	heal	pea	leak	ream
read	least	heat	gear	meal	sea	peak	seam
	yeast	meat	hear	peal	tea	teak	team
		neat	near	real		weak	cream
ean	**eap**	peat	rear	seal		bleak	dream
bean	heap	seat	tear	teal		creak	gleam
dean	leap	bleat	year	veal		sneak	scream
jeans	reap	cheat	clear	zeal		speak	steam
lean	cheap	cleat	shear	squeal		squeak	stream
mean		pleat	smear	steal		streak	
wean		treat	spear				
clean		wheat					

Words with *ee* Phonograms

eet	ee	eel	een	eed	eep	eek	eem
beet	bee	feel	seen	deed	deep	leek	deem
feet	fee	heel	teen	feed	jeep	meek	seem
meet	see	keel	green	heed	keep	peek	teem
fleet	tee	peel	sheen	need	peep	seek	
greet	wee	reel	queen	reed	seep	week	
sheet	flee	creel	screen	seed	weep	cheek	**eer**
sleet	free	kneel		weed	creep	creek	beer
street	glee	steel		bleed	cheep	Greek	deer
sweet	knee	wheel		breed	sleep	sleek	jeer
tweet	three			creed	steep		peer
	tree			freed	sweep		sneer
				greed			steer
				speed			
				steed			
				treed			

Words with *oa* Phonograms

oat	oast	oad	oach	oak	oal	oam	oan
boat	boast	load	coach	oak	coal	foam	loan
coat	coast	road	poach	soak	foal	loam	moan
goat	roast	toad	roach	cloak	goal	roam	groan
moat	toast			croak	shoal		
bloat							
float							
throat							

Phonics Skills Charts (continued)

Words with *oo* Phonograms

oon	oo	ool	oom	oot	ood	oop
boon	boo	cool	boom	boot	food	coop
moon	coo	fool	doom	coot	mood	goop
noon	goo	pool	loom	loot	brood	hoop
soon	moo	drool	room	moot		loop
croon	too	spool	zoom	root		droop
spoon	woo	stool	bloom	toot		scoop
swoon	zoo	school	broom	shoot		sloop
	shoo		gloom	snoot		snoop
			groom			swoop
						troop

Words with *ow* Phonograms

ow	own
bow	own
low	sown
mow	blown
row	flown
sow	grown
tow	known
blow	shown
flow	
glow	
grow	
know	
show	
slow	
snow	
stow	

Words with *oo* Phonograms

ook	ood
book	good
cook	hood
hook	wood
look	stood
took	
brook	
crook	
shook	

Words with *oi* Phonograms

oil	oin
boil	coin
coil	join
foil	loin
soil	groin
toil	
spoil	

Words with *oy*

boy	loyal	annoy
coy	royal	destroy
joy	oyster	employ
soy		enjoy
toy		
cloy		
ploy		

Words with *ou* Phonograms

ouse	out	ound	oud	ount
douse	bout	bound	loud	count
house	gout	found	cloud	fount
louse	lout	hound	proud	mount
mouse	pout	mound		fountain
blouse	rout	pound		mountain
grouse	tout	round		
	about	sound		
	grout	wound		
	shout	around		
	spout	ground		
	stout	astound		
	trout			
	sprout			

Phonics Skills Charts (continued)

Words with *ow* Phonograms

ow	own	ower	owel	owl
bow	down	bower	towel	cowl
cow	gown	cower	vowel	fowl
how	town	dower	trowel	howl
now	brown	power		jowl
row	clown	tower		owl
sow	crown	flower		growl
vow	drown	glower		prowl
wow	frown	shower		scowl
chow				
plow				
prow				
scow				

Words with *ar* Phonograms

ar	ark	ard	art	arm	arn	arp
bar	bark	card	cart	farm	barn	carp
car	dark	hard	dart	harm	darn	harp
far	hark	yard	mart	charm	yarn	tarp
jar	lark	guard	part			sharp
mar	mark	shard	tart			
tar	park		chart			
char	shark		smart			
scar	spark		start			
spar	stark					
star						

Words with *ir* Phonograms

ir	irl	irt
fir	girl	dirt
sir	swirl	flirt
stir	twirl	shirt
	whirl	skirt
		squirt

Words with *er* Phonograms

erb	erd	erk	erm
herb	herd	jerk	germ
verb	nerd	perk	term

Words with *ur* Phonograms

ur	urt	urn	urse
cur	curt	burn	curse
fur	hurt	turn	nurse
blur	blurt	churn	purse
slur	spurt	spurn	
spur			

Words with *or* Phonograms

ork	ort	ord	orn	orch
cork	fort	cord	born	porch
fork	port	ford	corn	torch
pork	short	lord	horn	scorch
York	snort	chord	torn	
stork	sport	sword	worn	
			scorn	
			sworn	
			thorn	

Appendix C

Frameworks for Classroom Instruction

Much has been learned in the past twenty years about how to teach children to read and write. The importance of literacy learning is such that we look for teaching methods that are based in scientific research. We also look for ways to teach that engage children and make their work in classrooms enjoyable. The two frameworks for classroom instruction have been developed by the Foundation for California Early Literacy Learning and are used as part of a professional development program. One framework focuses on pre-Kindergarten through grade 3, and the second extends the same methods into grades 4 through 8. These frameworks were developed to support teaching that uses literacy as a primary method of instruction. These teaching methods are both supported in the research and known to teachers as best practice.

Framework for Classroom Instruction
Pre-Kindergarten - Grade 3

Element	Values	Supporting Research
Oral Language	Assists students in language acquisition. Develops and increases vocabulary. Promotes the use of accurate language structure. Uses oral language to access reading and writing.	Bruner (1983) Cazden (1992) Chomsky (1972) Ferreiro (1982) Holdaway (1979) Wells (1986)
Phonological Skills	Builds a foundation of phonemic awareness for explicit skills learning. Teaches systematic phonics through writing, spelling, and reading. Supports development of accurate spelling.	Adams (1998) Bear, Invernizzi, Templeton, & Johnston (1996) Kirk, Kirk & Minskoff (1985) Shook, Klein, & Swartz (1998)
Read Aloud	Builds vocabulary. Introduces good children's literature through a variety of genre. Increases repertoire of language and its use.	Adams (1990) Clark (1976) Cochran -Smith (1984) Cohen (1968) Durkin (1966) Goodman, Y. (1984) Green & Harker (1982) Hiebert (1988) Huck Hickman, & Hepler (1994) Ninio (1980) Pappas & Brown (1987) Schickendanz (1978) Wells (1985)

Element	Values	Supporting Research
Shared Reading	Promotes the development of early reading strategies. Encourages cooperative learning and child-to-child support. Stresses phonemic awareness and phonological skills.	Holdaway (1979) Martinez & Roser (1985) Pappas & Brown (1987 Rowe (1987) Snow (1983) Sulzby (1985) Teale & Suizby (1986)
Guided Reading	Allows observation of strategic reading in selected novel texts. Provides direct instruction of problem-solving strategies. Allows for classroom intervention of reading difficulties.	Clay (1991a & 1991b) Fountas & Pinnell (1996) Holdaway (1979) Lyons, Pinnell & DeFord (1993) McKenzie (1986) Routman (1991) Wong, Groth & O'Flahavan (1994)
Independent Reading	Allows children to practice strategies being learned. Develops fluency using familiar texts. Encourages successful problem-solving.	Clay (1991a) McKenzie (1986) Taylor (1993)
Interactive Writing	Provides an opportunity to jointly plan and construct text. Develops letter-sound correspondence and spelling. Teaches phonics.	Button, Johnson & Furgerson (1996) McCarrier, Fountas, & Pinnell (2000) Pinnell & McCarrier (1994) Swartz, Klein, & Shook (2001)
Independent Writing	Encourages writing for different purposes and different audiences. Fosters creativity and an ability to compose.	Bissex (1980) Clay (1975) Dyson (1982; 1988) Ferreiro & Teberosky (1982) Goodman, Y. (1984) Harste, Woodward, & Burke (1984)

Element	Values	Supporting Research
Phonological Skills	Directly and systematically teaches essential skills. Uses oral language to access reading and writing. Builds a foundation of explicit skills learning. Teaches systematic phonics through writing, spelling, and reading. Supports the development of accurate spelling.	Adams (1991); Blau (1998); Brady & Moats (1997); Cunningham & Stanovich (1998); Cunningham (1990); Duffelmeyer & Black (1996); Foorman, Francis, Shaywitz, Shaywitz, & Fletcher (1997); Fry (1997); Fry (1998); Liberman, Shankweiler, & Liberman (1989); Lowe & Walters (1991); Lyon & Moats (1997); McPike (1995); Moats (1994); Morris, Ervin, & Conrad (1996); Shaywitz (1996); Stanovich (1993); Tierney (1998); Torgesen (1998); Torgesen, Wagner, & Rashotte (1997); Triplett & Stahl (1998); Wolfe (1998)
Read Aloud	Expands concept development and language structure. Fluent, expressive reading New and familiar concepts and context Language and grammar usage	Andrews (1998); Barrentine (1996); Schickendanz (1978)
Shared Reading	Increases fluency and extends phonological awareness. Phonological awareness for explicit skills learning. Choral reading Reader's theater	Beck, McKeown, & Ormanson (1997); Blum & Koskinen (1991); Clark (1995); Dowhower (1991); Hasbrouck & Tindal (1992); Miller (1998); Nathan & Stanovich (1991); Samuels (1997); Samuels, Schermer, & Reinking (1992); Tangel & Blachman (1995)
Directed Reading	Provides explicit skills and comprehension instruction for readers at various ability levels, integrates reading into the content areas, and teaches study and reference skills. Guided reading Reciprocal teaching Literature circles	Beck, McKeown, Hamilton, & Kucan (1998); Brown & Cambourne (1990); Chomsky (1975); Fletcher & Lyon (1998); Gilliam, Pena, & Mountain (1980); Jones, Coombs, & McKinney (1994); Juel (1998); Klein (1981); Klein (1996); Klein (1997); Lee & Neal (1993); Moats, Pearson, Roehler, Dole, & Duffy (1992); Perfetti (1995); Shanklin & Rhodes (1989); Showers, Joyce, Scanlon, & Schnaubelt (1998); Stahl & Shiel (1992); Tomlinson & Kalbfeisch (1998); Weir (1998)

Element	Values	Supporting Research
Independent Reading	Allows for extended practice, increased comprehension, and higher-order thinking skills. Specific reading strategies and text organization Content area study	Anderson (1996); Henk & Melnick (1995); Metzger (1998)
Directed Writing	Supports the accurate construction of text and effective spelling strategies. Interactive writing and interactive editing Writer's workshop	Ehri (1998); Fletcher & Lyon (1998); Foorman, Francis, Fletcher, Schatschneider, & Metha (1998); Greene (1998); Heald-Taylor (1998); Henry (1988); Invernizzi, Abouzeid, & Bloodgood (1997); Juel (1988); Moats (1998); Swartz, Klein, & Shook (2001); Zutell (1996)
Independent Writing	Encourages creativity and the ability to write for different purposes. Language structure and correct grammar usage Accurate spelling and punctuation skills	Cassady (1998); Dyson (1982; 1988); Ferreiro & Teberosky (1982); National Center on Education and the Economy and the University of Pittsburgh (1999)
Oral Presentation	Formalizes the process of sharing ideas and reporting information. Content area oral reports Oral interpretation of literature Drama/performance	Bruner (1983); California Department of Education (1998); Cazden (1992); Chomsky (1972); Ferreiro & Teberosky (1982); Klein (1997)

Big Books from Dominie Press

Fiction

Carousel Readers

All Kinds of Food
All Kinds of Homes
Bath for Patches, A
Butch, the Outdoor Cat
Clock That Couldn't Tell Time, The
Dad's Great Big Fish
Day Our Teacher Lost Her Voice, The
Diana Made Dinner
Fisherman Fred
I See Circles
I'm Sick Today
Mathematical Stew
Mr. Cricket Finds a Friend
My Dad Cooks
My Picture
Party Smarty
Ride in the Country, A
Shapes
What Is Green?
When I Say …

Phonics Readers

Bill's Trip
Fox's Box
It's Broken
Lumpy Rug
Mike's Bike
Music Students
Pete's Peacock
Playing Games
Sam's Cap
Ted's Letter

Cambridge

Afloat in a Boat
All By Myself
Big Book of Number Rhymes
Big Book of Nursery Rhymes
Chinese New Year, The
Clever Tortoise
Dirty Dog
Elves and the Shoemaker, The
Five Green Monsters
Goldilocks and the Three Bears
Hide and Seek
I Went to School This Morning
Let's Pretend
Lick of the Spoon, A
My Pet
Nonsense!
One Teddy All Alone
Out and About
Picnic, The
Planet Ocky: Ham & Jam
Planet Ocky: Jump & Bump
Runaway Chapati, The
Three Fat Cats
Tiger Dreams
Two Babies
Very Hot Day, A
Walking in the Jungle
Wayne's Box
What Am I?
What For?
What's in the Box?
What's the Time?
Wiggle and Giggle

Nonfiction

Factivity

Busy People Everywhere!
Changes in the Earth and Sky
Happy Birthday, America!
How Does It Move?
Life Cycles
Living Things
Look at This!
My World, Our World
Objects in the Sky
Our Grandparents' World and Ours
Places to Live
Planet Earth
Round and Round
Sharing Good Times around the World
Switch On!
This Is Our World
What Do I Do in a Day?

Big Alphabet Book, The

Cambridge

Bubbles
Camouflage
Coral Reef
Dinosaur
Tomb of Nebamun, The

Glossary

Adjective. The part of speech that modifies a noun.

Adverb. The part of speech that modifies a verb, adjective, or another adverb.

Alliteration. Repetition of initial sounds in several words or in a phrase or longer stretch of text.

Alphabetic principle. The concept underlying writing systems that each phoneme/sound should have its own grapheme/letter.

Analogy. General similarity in word components or meaning.

Anchor word. An automatically known word in a text that helps speed the reading along.

Anecdotal records. A teacher's notes from observing a student's reading and/or writing behaviors; sometimes includes samples of a student's work.

Background knowledge. Information that readers and writers bring to a task, based on what they already know or have experienced.

Blending. Combining of sounds in two or more letters.

Breaking down. Examining or analyzing a word, phrase, or sentence in all of its components: letters, sounds, spelling pattern, and sentence structure.

Building up. Combining sounds, letters, and spelling patterns to make words, phrases, or sentences.

Cause and effect. An event or interaction and its related outcome.

Chunk. Usually referring to a group of sounds/letters, including the syllable unit, prefix, suffix, onset, rhyme, and phonograms.

Clarify. To seek or provide further information, such as the meaning of a word or idea.

Comprehension strategies. Techniques used in understanding the meaning or importance of a passage; includes determining importance and questioning ideas.

Concepts about print. Basic elements of reading, including book handling, directionality, reading the punctuation, recognizing letters and words, and matching sound to letter.

Connections. Relating to a text by linking what readers bring from themselves and their feelings, from other texts, and from their experiences in the world.

Context(ual) clues. Words surrounding an unknown term or concept that can help the reader define that term or concept.

Conventions. Standard patterns used in writing, such as spelling conventions, punctuation, and grammar.

Correction tape. Any type of blank tape that can cover an error and be written on to make a correction.

Cross-check. To compare one piece of information against another; for example, to compare a picture and a word for that picture.

Decode. To analyze spoken or written symbols of a language in order to understand their intended meaning.

Digraph. Two letters that represent one speech sound.

Diphthong. A single vowel sound made from two vowel sounds in a syllable.

Directionality. The ability to perceive and use spatial orientation accurately.

Early reading strategies. The earliest "in the head" understandings a child uses to begin processing in reading and writing; these include directionality, one-to-one matching, and locating known and unknown words.

Edit. To correct or adjust an existing text to make a better piece of writing or to change the type of writing, such as changing genres.

Encode. To change a message into written symbols.

Expository writing. A traditional form of composition designed to explain or set forth a point.

Extension activities. Suggestions for extending a lesson in a connected way.

Familiar text. A previously read text at the instructional or independent level.

Figurative language. Various figures of speech, such as metaphors and similes.

Fluency. The ability to read with phrasing and expression.

Genre. A category system for classifying text, usually by form or content.

Grammar. A system of rules implicit in a language, including word formation and inflections; standards for language use.

High frequency words. Words that occur very often in spoken or written language.

Highlighter tape. Transparent tape that is used to point out a word; similar to a highlighter pen in purpose.

Homonyms. Words that have the same sound and usually the same spelling but mean different things; for example, bat as in the animal, and bat as in baseball.

Homophones. Words that mean different things but are pronounced the same; for example, knight and night.

Idiom. A phrase that is understood differently than the literal meaning.

Inferring. Drawing a conclusion from facts or information in a reading passage.

Inflectional ending. A suffix that changes the form or function of a root word, stem, or compound, but not its basic meaning.

Instructional purpose. The intent of the lesson, based on content standards and student needs.

Interactive editing. A teaching method in which teacher and children work together to edit familiar, error-free text. The reciprocity of reading and writing is a key feature of interactive editing.

Interactive writing. A teaching method in which children and teacher negotiate what they are going to write and then share the pen to construct the message.

Irregular word. A word that does not follow a regular linguistic pattern or rule for its spelling or pronunciation.

Key content words. Terms in the reading or text that carry the basic information; usually 15-18% of the words in an average content area passage.

Known word. A word that is known in reading and/or writing. Known words can be sight words or decodable words that are automatically recognized.

Language structure. A system including the rules for combining components, specifically, words; the way in which words are combined to form a language.

Literacy center. A set of materials used for independent practice of a taught skill. Literacy centers are used in classrooms as a way of managing small group reading activities.

Literary elements. Relating to or dealing with an element of a book or written materials.

Locate (as a strategy). To find a word in a text, based on the sound/letter sequence.

Magna Doodle®. A commercial product used to write examples to support the teaching of interactive writing; uses a blunt instrument and board with magnetic shavings to form letters.

Masking card. An index card or piece of oaktag strip or construction paper that is used to cover a word or a line of text.

Metaphor. An implicit comparison between two things, or having an object symbolize another object or idea.

Modifier. A word, phrase, or clause that modifies, changes, or adds to the meaning of another word, phrase, or clause.

Name chart. A classroom chart of the students' first and sometimes last names used to support phonics and spelling instruction in constructing interactive writing messages; in upper grades this might take the form of a list of presidents or other names.

Narrative writing. An account of a story, retelling or highlighting the main events.

One-to-one matching. The ability of a reader to match one word said to one word read; an early reading skill.

Onset. Usually the consonants preceding the vowel of a syllable.

Paraphrase. Restating the meaning of something spoken or written.

Persuasive writing. A style of writing used to convince a person to take an action or accept a point of view.

Phonemic awareness. The awareness of the sounds (phonemes) that make up spoken words.

Phonics. A method of teaching reading and spelling that stresses the sound/symbol relationship.

Phonogram. In word recognition, a sequence including a vowel and one or more ending consonants.

Phonological awareness. The awareness of the constituent sounds of words in learning to read and spell.

Phonology. The study of speech sounds and their function in a language.

Phrasing. Grouping words together for reading fluency, usually based on phrase units or the subject and predicate of a sentence; may be different in reading poetry.

Predicate. In grammar, the part of a sentence that expresses something about the subject; often called a verb phrase.

Prepositional phrase. A word phrase that includes a preposition and its object; usually used as an adjective or adverb.

Prompt. Language used by the teacher to draw the student's attention to a particular aspect of the reading process.

R-controlled vowels. Vowels that undergo a change in sound due to the r sound that follows them.

Read aloud. Sharing a story aloud, developing vocabulary, modeling structure and fluency, and introducing content.

Reader's Theater. A style of play reading that involves the use of scripts and limited actions or costumes.

Reciprocal teaching. A teaching strategy whereby teacher and students share the responsibility for conducting a discussion.

Reciprocity of reading and writing. The concept that reading and writing are supportive processes, and that each one is learned more effectively by relating it to the other.

Return sweep. Occurs when the eyes reach the end of a line of print and move to the beginning of the next line on the same page.

Rhyme. Usually identical, or sometimes very similar, recurring final sounds in words.

Rime. A vowel and any following consonants of a syllable.

Segmentation. Dividing a word into its constituent phonemes.

Self-correcting. Occurs when a reader or writer notices an error and corrects it without assistance.

Self-monitoring. Noticing when there is an error in reading or writing text.

Shared reading. A teaching method in which the teacher and children read together from text that is visible to all.

Simile. A figure of speech comparing two different things, usually using like or as.

Skill. Learning a specific task or item, such as writing a letter name or recalling a sight word.

Spelling pattern. The sequence of letters (consonants and vowels) that form a pattern for spelling a word; for example, CVC and CVVC patterns.

Strategy. Organizing a group of items, such as letters, names, or sight words, into a way of learning that is generative.

Stretching words. Articulating a word slowly and distinctly in order to hear the component (segmented) sounds.

Subject. In grammar, the main topic of a sentence to which the predicate refers.

Substitution. The use of one word in place of another; usually considered a type of error in reading.

Summary statement. A bringing together of the key information in a passage.

Synonym. A word or phrase having the same, or almost the same, meaning as another word or phrase.

Synthesize. To draw ideas together into a form of a summary.

Text structure. The format of a story, poem, or nonfiction book, such as a repeated pattern text.

Think aloud. To model thinking behaviors for students by talking through a process as it is happening, such as a think aloud during the reading of a story to a class.

Venn diagram. Overlapping circles used two show similarities and differences in semantic mapping.

Visualize. To form a mental image of a word or an object.

Wikki Stix®. A commercially made product using wax-covered string that can be used to highlight letters, words, parts of speech, punctuation, etc.

Word analysis. A general label for analyzing words into their constituent parts, including recognition of sight words; becomes progressively more difficult in polysyllabic words.

Word bank. A resource of words to be used for reading, writing, or spelling.

Word play. An opportunity for students to explore words by rhyming or making up nonsense words; useful for word analysis.

Word wall. The use of print on walls that includes various types organized for instruction, such as high frequency words, word families or rhyming words, and content area words; often used in a reduced form as a writing resource at a student's desk.

Word window. A device used to show only a portion of a sentence, usually one word or phrase; most often made of cardboard or see-through tape.

Written language conventions. The accepted norms of writing, in both structure and punctuation.

Bibliography

Adams, M. (1990). *Beginning to Read: Thinking and Learning about Print.* Cambridge, MA: MIT Press.

Adams, M. (1998). *Phonemic Awareness in Young Children.* Baltimore, MA: Paul H.Brookes Publishing Co.

Anderson, R.C. (1996). *Research Foundations to Support Wide Reading.* In Creany, V. (Ed.), *Promoting Reading in Developing Countries*, (pp. 44-77). Newark, DE: International Reading Association.

Andrews, S.E. (1998). "Using Inclusion Literature to Promote Positive Attitudes toward Disabilities." *Journal of Adolescent & Adult Literacy*, 41(6), (pp. 420-426).

Barrentine, S.J. (1996). "Engaging with Reading through Interactive Read-alouds." *The Reading Teacher*, 50(1), (pp. 36-43).

Bear, D., Invernizzi, M., Templeton, S., & Johnston, F. (1996). *Words Their Way.* Upper Saddle River, NJ: Prentice-Hall, Inc.

Beck, I., McKeown, M.G., Hamilton, R.L., & Kucan, L. (1998, Spring). "Getting at the Meaning." *American Educator*, 22(1), (pp. 66-85).

Beck, I., McKeown, M.G., & Ormanson, R.C. (1997). *The Effects and Uses of Diverse*

Vocabulary Instructional Techniques. In McKeown, M.G. & Curtis, M.E. (Eds.), *The Nature of Vocabulary Acquisition*, (pp. 147-163). Hillsdale, NJ: Erlbaum.

Bissex, G. (1980). *GNYS at Work: A Child Learns to Write and Read.* Cambridge, MA:Harvard University Press.

Blau, S. (1998, February). "Toward the Separation of School and State." *Language Arts*, 75(2), (pp. 132-136).

Blum, I.H., & Koskinen, P.S. (1991, Summer). "Repeated Reading: A Strategy for Enhancing Fluency and Fostering Expertise." *Theory Into Practice*, 30, (pp. 195-200).

Brady, S., & Moats, L.C. (1997). *Informed Instruction for Reading Success: Foundations for Teacher Preparation.* Baltimore, MD: Orton Dyslexia Society.

Brown, H., & Cambourne, B. (1990). *The 'What', 'How' and 'Why' of the Retelling Procedure. Read and Retell: A Strategy for the Whole-language/Natural Learning Classroom.* Portsmouth, NH: Heinemann.

Bruner, J.S. (1983). *Child's Talk: Learning to Use Language.* London: W.W. Norton & Co.

Button, K., Johnson, M.J., & Furgerson, P. (1996). "Interactive Writing in a Primary Classroom." *The Reading Teacher*, 49(6), (pp. 446-454).

California Department of Education. (1998). *English Language Arts Content Standards for California Public Schools.* Sacramento, CA.

Cassady, J.K. (1998). "Wordless Books: No-risk Tools for Inclusive Middle-grade Classrooms." *Journal of Adolescent & Adult Literacy*, 41(6), (pp. 428-432).

Cazden, C.B. (1992). *Whole Language Plus, Essays on Literacy in the United States and New Zealand.* New York: Teacher's College Press.

Chomsky, C. (1976). "After Decoding: What?" *Language Arts*, 53(3), (pp 288-96, 314).

Chomsky, C. (1972). "Stages in Language Development and Reading Exposure." *Harvard Educational Review*, 42(1), (pp. 1-33).

Clark, M.M. (1976). *Young Fluent Readers: What Can They Teach Us?* London: Heinemann.

Clark, C.H. (1995). "Teaching Students about Reading: A Fluency Example." *Reading Horizons*, 35(3), (pp. 250-266).

Clay, M.M. (1975). *What Did I Write?* Portsmouth, NH: Heinemann.

Clay, M.M. (1991a). *Becoming Literate: The Construction of Inner Control.* Auckland, NZ: Heinemann.

Clay, M.M. (1991b, December). "Introducing a New Storybook to Young Readers." *The Reading Teacher*, 45, (pp. 264-273).

Cochran-Smith, M. (1984). *The Making of a Reader.* Norwood, NJ: Ablex.

Cohen, D. (1968). "The Effects of Literature on Vocabulary and Reading Achievement." *Elementary English*, 45, (pp. 209-213, 217).

Cunningham, A.E., & Stanovich, K.E. (1998, Spring). "What Reading Does for the Mind." *American Educator*, 22(1), (pp. 8-15).

Cunningham, P. (1990, October). "The Names Test: A Quick Assessment of Decoding Ability." *The Reading Teacher*, 44(2), (pp. 124-129).

Dowhower, S.L. (1991, Summer). "Speaking of Prosody: Fluency's Unattended Bedfellow." *Theory Into Practice*, 30, (pp. 124-129).

Duffelmeyer, F.A., & Black, J.L. (1996, October). "The Names Test: A Domain-specific Validation Study." *The Reading Teacher*, 50(2), (pp. 148-150).

Durkin, D. (1966). *Children Who Read Early.* New York: Teacher's College Press.

Dyson, A.H. (1982). "Reading, Writing and Language: Young Children Solve the Written Language Puzzle." *Language Arts*, 59, (pp. 829-839).

Dyson, A.H. (1988). "Negotiating among Multiple Worlds: The Space/Time Dimensions of Young Children's Composing." *Research in the Teaching of English*, 22(4), (pp. 355-390).

Ehri, L.C. (1998). "The Development of Spelling Knowledge and Its Role in Reading Acquisition and Reading Disability." *Journal of Reading Disabilities*, 22(6), (pp. 356-365).

Ferreiro, E., & Teberosky, A. (1982). *Literacy before Schooling*. Portsmouth, NH: Heinemann.

Fletcher, J., & Lyon, R. (1998). *Reading: A Research-based Approach*. In W. Evers (Ed.), *What's Gone Wrong in America's Classrooms*. Palo Alto, CA: Hoover Institution Press, Stanford University.

Foorman, B.R., Francis, D.J., Fletcher, J.M., Schatschneider, C., & Metha, P. (1998). "The Role of Instruction in Learning to Read: Preventing Reading Failure in At-risk Children." *Journal of Educational Psychology*, 90, (pp. 1-15).

Foorman, B.R., Francis, D.J., Shaywitz, S.E., Shaywitz, B., & Fletcher, J.M. (1997). *The Case for Early Reading Intervention*. In B. Blachman (Ed.), *Foundations of Reading Acquisition: Implications for Intervention and Dyslexia*. Hillsdale, NJ: Lawrence Erlbaum.

Fountas, I., & Pinnell, G.S. (1996). *Guided Reading*. Portsmouth, NH: Heinemann.

Fry, E. (1998). "An Open Letter to United States President Clinton." *The Reading Teacher*, 51(5), (pp. 366-370).

Fry, E. (1997). *Comprehensive Phonics Charts*. Phonics Charts. California: Laguna Beach Educational Books.

Gilliam, F., Pena, S., & Mountain, L. (1980, January). "The Fry Graph Applied to Spanish Readability." *The Reading Teacher*, (pp. 426-430).

Goodman, Y. (1984). *The Development of Initial Literacy*. In H. Goelman, A. Oberg, & F. Smith (Eds.), *Awakening to Literacy*. Portsmouth, NH: Heinemann.

Greene, J.F. (1998, Spring/Summer). "Another Chance." *American Educator*, 22(1), (pp. 74-79).

Green, J.L., & Harker, J.O. (1982). *Reading to Children: A Communicative Process*. In J.A. Langer & M. T. Smith-Burke (Eds.). *Reader Meets Author/Bridging the Gap: A Psycholinguistic and Sociolinguistic Perspective*, (pp. 196-221). Newark, DE: International Reading Association.

Harste, J.E., Woodward, V.A., & Burke, C.L. (1984). *Language Stories and Literacy Lessons*. (pp. 49-76). Portsmouth, NH: Heinemann.

Hasbrouck, J.E., & Tindal, G. (1992, Spring). "Curriculum-based Oral Reading Fluency Norms for Students in Grades 2 through 5." *Teaching Exceptional Children*, 24, (pp. 41-44).

Heald-Taylor, B.G. (1998, February). "Three Paradigms of Spelling Instruction in Grades 3 to 6." *The Reading Teacher*, 51(5), (pp. 404-413).

Henk, W.A., & Melnick, S.A. (1995, March). "The Reader Self-Perception Scale (RSPS): A New Tool for Measuring How Children Feel about Themselves as Readers." *The Reading Teacher*, 48(6), (pp. 470-483).

Henry, M.K. (1988). "Beyond Phonics: Integrated Decoding and Spelling Instruction Based on Word Origin and Structure." *Annals of Dyslexia*, 38, (pp. 258-275).

Hiebert, E.H. (1988, November). "The Role of Literacy Experiences in Early Childhood Programs." *Elementary School Journal*, 89, (pp. 161-171).

Holdaway, D. (1979). *The Foundations of Literacy*. Sydney, Australia: Ashton Scholastic.

Huck, C., Hepler, S., & Hickman, J. (1994). *Children's Literature in the Elementary School*. Madison, WI: Brown & Benchmark.

Invernizzi, M.A., Abouzeid, M.P., & Bloodgood, J.W. (1997, March). "Integrated Word Study: Spelling, Grammar, and Meaning in the Language Arts Classroom." *Language Arts*, 74, (pp. 185-192).

Jones, H.J., Coombs, W.T., & McKinney, C.W. (1994). "A Themed Literature Unit Versus a Textbook: A Comparison of the Effects on Content Acquisition and Attitudes in Elementary Social Studies." *Reading Research and Instruction*, 34(2), (pp. 85-96).

Juel, C. (1988). "Learning to Read and Write: A Longitudinal Study of 54 Children from First through Fourth Grades." *Journal of Educational Psychology*, 80(4), (pp. 437-447).

Kirk, S., Kirk, W., & Minskoff, E. (1985). *Phonic Remedial Reading Lessons*. Novata, CA: Academic Therapy Publications.

Klein, A.F. (1997). *Advanced Directed Writing Activities*. Redlands, CA: Foundation for California Early Literacy Learning.

Klein, A.F. (1996). *Directed Writing Activities*. Redlands, CA: Foundation for California Early Literacy Learning.

Klein, A.F. (1981). *Test Taking Strategies for the Middle Grades*. Redlands, CA: Foundation for California Early Literacy Learning.

Lee, N., & Neal, J.C. (1993). "Reading Rescue: Intervention for a Student 'At Promise.'" *Journal of Reading*, 36(4), (pp. 276-282).

Liberman, I.Y., Shankweiler, D., & Liberman (Eds.) (1989). *Phonology and Reading Disability: Solving the Reading Puzzle*. Ann Arbor, MI: University of Michigan Press.

Lowe, K., & Walters, J. (1991). *The Unsuccessful Reader: Negotiating New Perceptions. The Literacy Agenda*. (pp. 114-136). Portsmouth, NH: Heinemann.

Lowery, L. (1998, November). "How New Science Curriculums Reflect Brain Research." *Educational Leadership*, 56(3), (pp. 26-30).

Lyon, G.R., & Moats, L.C. (1997, November/December). "Critical Conceptual and Methodological Considerations in Reading Intervention Research." *Journal of Learning Disabilities*, 30, (pp. 578-588).

Lyons, C.A., Pinnell, G.S., & DeFord, D.E. (1993). *Partners in Learning: Teachers and Children in Reading Recovery®.* New York: Teachers College Press.

Martinez, M., & Roser N. (1985, April). "Read it Again: The Value of Repeated Readings during Storytime." *Reading Teacher,* (38), (pp. 782-786).

McCarrier, A., Fountas, I., Pinnell, G. (2000). *Interactive Writing: How Language and Literacy Come Together.* Portsmouth, NH: Heinemann.

McKenzie (1986). *Journeys into Literacy.* Huddersfield, England: Schofield & Sims.

McPike, E. (1995, Summer). "Learning to Read: Schooling's First Mission." *American Educator,* (pp. 3-6).

Metzger, M. (1998, November). "Teaching Reading: Beyond the Plot." *Phi Delta Kappan.* 80(3), (pp. 240-246, 256).

Miller, T. (1998, February). "The Place of Picture Books in Middle-level Classrooms." *Journal of Adolescent & Adult Literacy,* 41(5), (pp. 376-381).

Moats, L.C. (1998). *Reading, Spelling, and Writing Disabilities in the Middle Grades.* In B. Wong (Ed.), *Learning About Learning Disabilities.* San Diego, CA: Academic Press.

Moats, L.C. (1994). "The Missing Foundation in Teacher Education: Knowledge of the Structure of Spoken and Written Language." *Annals of Dyslexia: An Interdisciplinary Journal of the Orton Dyslexia Society,* 44, (p. 81).

Morris, D., Ervin, C., & Conrad, K. (1996, February). "A Case Study of Middle School Reading Disability." *The Reading Teacher,* 49(5), (pp. 368-376).

Nathan, R.G., & Stanovich, K.E. (1991, Summer). "The Causes and Consequences of Differences in Reading Fluency." *Theory Into Practice,* 30, (pp. 176-184).

National Center of Education and the Economy and the University of Pittsburgh. (1999). *Reading and Writing Grade by Grade: Primary Literacy Standards for Kindergarten through Third Grade.*

Ninio, A. (1980). "Picture-book Reading in Mother-Infant Dyads belonging to Two Subgroups in Israel." *Child Development,* 51, (pp. 587-590).

Pappas, C.C., & Brown, E. (1987, May). "Learning to Read by Reading: Learning How to Extend the Functional Potential of Language." *Research in the Teaching of English,* 21, (pp. 160-184).

Pearson, P.D., Roehler, L.R., Dole, J.A., & Duffy, G.G. (1992). *Developing Expertise in Reading Comprehension.* In Samuels, S.J., & Farstrup, A.E. (Eds.), *What Research Says to the Teachers,* (pp. 145-199). Newark, DE: International Reading Association.

Perfetti, C. (1995). "Cognitive Research Can Inform Reading Education." *Journal of Research in Reading,* 18, (pp. 106-115).

Pinnell, G.S., & McCarrier, A. (1994). *Interactive Writing: A Transition Tool for Assisting Children in Learning to Read and Write.* In E. Heibert & B. Taylor (Eds.). *Getting Reading Right from the Start: Effective Early Literacy Interventions.* Needham Heights, MA: Allyn & Bacon.

Routman, R. (1991). *Invitations.* Portsmouth, NH: Heinemann.

Rowe, D.W. (1987). "Literacy Learning as an Intertextual Process." *National Reading Conference Yearbook,* 36, (pp. 101-112).

Samuels, S.J. (1997, February). "The Method of Repeated Readings." *The Reading Teacher,* 50(5), (pp. 376-384).

Samuels, S.J., Schermer, N., & Reinking, D. (1992). *Reading Fluency: Techniques for Making Decoding Automatic.* In S. Samuels and A. Farstrup (Eds.), *What Research Has to Say about Reading Instruction,* (pp. 124-144). Newark, DE: International Reading Association.

Schickendanz, J. (1978). "'Please Read That Story Again!' Exploring Relationships between Story Reading and Learning to Read." *Young Children,* 33(5), (pp. 98-104).

Shanklin, N.L., & Rhodes, L.K. (1989, March). "Comprehension Instruction as Sharing and Extending." *The Reading Teacher,* 42, (pp. 496-500).

Shaywitz, S.E. (1996). "Dyslexia." *Scientific American,* 275(5), (pp. 98-104).

Showers, B., Joyce, B., Scanlon, M., & Schnaubelt, C. (1998, March). "A Second Chance to Learn to Read." *Educational Leadership,* 55(6), (pp. 27-30).

Snow, C.E. (1983). "Literacy and Language: Relationships during the Preschool Years." *Harvard Educational Review,* 53(2), (pp. 165-189).

Stahl, S.A., & Shiel, T.G. (1992). "Teaching Meaning Vocabulary: Productive Approaches for Poor Readers." *Reading and Writing Quarterly: Overcoming Learning Disabilities,* 8, (pp. 223-241).

Stanovich, K.E. (1993, December). "Romance and Reality." *The Reading Teacher,* 47(4), (pp. 280-290).

Sulzby, E. (1985). "Children's Emergent Reading of Favorite Storybooks: A Developmental Study." *Reading Research Quarterly,* 20(4), (pp. 458-481).

Swartz, S.L., Klein, A.F., & Shook, R.E. (2001). *Interactive Writing and Interactive Editing.* Carlsbad, CA: Dominie Press.

Swartz, S.L., Shook, R.E., & Klein, A.F. (1998). *California Early Literacy Learning (CELL) (Technical Report).* Redlands, CA: Foundation for California Early Literacy Learning.

Bibliography (continued...)

Tangel, D., & Blachman, B. (1995, June). "Effect of Phoneme Awareness Instruction on the Invented Spellings of First Grade Children: A One-year Follow-up." *Journal of Reading Behavior*, 27, (pp. 153-185).

Taylor, D. (1993). *From the Child's Point of View.* Portsmouth, NH: Heinemann.

Teale, W.H., & Sulzby, E. (Eds.). (1986). *Emergent Literacy: Writing and Reading.* Norwood, NJ: Ablex.

Tierney, R.J. (1998, February). "Literacy Assessment Reform: Shifting Beliefs, Principled Possibilities, and Emerging Practices." *The Reading Teacher*, 51(5), (pp. 374-390).

Tomlinson, C.A., & Kalbfleisch, M.L. (1998, November). "Teach Me, Teach My Brain: A Call for Differentiated Classrooms." *Educational Leadership*, 56(3), (pp. 52-55).

Torgesen, J.K. (1998, Spring/Summer). "Catch Them before the Fall." *American Educator*, 22(1), (pp. 32-39).

Torgesen, J.K., Wagner, R.K., Y Rashotte, C.A. (1997). *Approaches to the Prevention and Remediation of Phonologically-based Disabilities.* In B. Blachman (Ed.), *Foundations of Reading Acquisition and Dyslexia: Implications for Early Intervention,* (pp. 287-304) Mahwah, NJ: Lawrence Erlbaum.

Triplett, C.F., & Stahl, S.A. (1998, Summer). "Words, Words, Words. Word Sorts: Maximizing Student Input in Work Study." *Illinois Reading Council Journal*, 26(3), (pp. 84-87).

Weir, C. (1998, March). "Using Embedded Questions to Jumpstart Metacognition in Middle School Remedial Readers." *Journal of Adolescent & Adult Literacy*, 41(6), (pp. 458-467).

Wells, C. (1986). *The Meaning Makers: Children Learning Language and Using Language to Learn.* Portsmouth, NH: Heinemann.

Wells, C.G. (1985). *Preschool Literacy-related Activities and Success in School.* In D. Olson, N. Torrance, & A. Hildyard (Eds.), *Literacy, Language, and Learning: The Nature and Consequences of Literacy,* (pp. 229-255). Cambridge, England: Cambridge University Press.

Wolfe, P. (1998, November). "Revisiting Effective Teaching." *Educational Leadership*, 56(3), (pp. 61-64).

Wong, S.D., Groth, L.A., & O'Flahavan, J.D. (1994). *Characterizing Teacher-student Interaction in Reading Recovery® Lessons.* Universities of Georgia and Maryland, National Reading Research Center Reading Research Report.

Zutell, J. (1996, October). "The Directed Spelling Thinking Activity (DSTA): Providing an Effective Balance in Work Study Instruction." *The Reading Teacher*, 50(2), (pp. 98-108).

Index